# Table of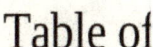

## III. Epilogue

# I.   INTRODUCTION

This book is a result of my very great passion for soundtracks and in particular for the music of Jerry Goldsmith, Bill Conti, Patrick Doyle, Hans Zimmer, John Williams and Elmer Bernstein to name just a few.

I have been listening to orchestral soundtracks since I was a child and was occasionally considered strange by my classmates. While they were listening to the latest pop songs by Madonna, a-ha, Michael Jackson, Tina Turner, David Bowie and Bruce Springsteen, I was falling in love with the music of an American film music composer who wrote for movies like *The Omen* (1976), *The Secret of NIMH* (1982), *First Blood* (1982), *Under Fire* (1983), *Supergirl* (1984), *Gremlins* (1984), *Explorers* (1985) and *Basic Instinct* (1992). Seriously?

But, like all passionate people, I carried on and looked for other people who were also excited by soundtracks. I discovered the Jerry Goldsmith Society and realised that Jerry Goldsmith gave annual concerts in London, my favourite European city and the place where I now work and live. So, I bought a ticket, flew to London, listened to Jerry Goldsmith for the first time live, and had one of the happiest moments of my life. If that isn't passion, I don't know what is!

## Passionate about Jerry Goldsmith

I discovered Jerry Goldsmith in 1989. Before that, I had been a fan of Bill Conti in particular and some John Barry soundtracks, but had not come across a composer I was really passionate about. When I first listened to Jerry Goldsmith's music, I was extremely excited by its rich orchestration, his sense of drama and his ability to support the emotions in even small scenes in a movie with his lovely melodies. For example, there is a short scene between Peter Weller and Amanda Pays in *Leviathan* (1989) where they have just a brief conversation lasting around just a few minutes, but that was enough time for Jerry Goldsmith to introduce a beautiful love theme. This scene is the only time the theme is heard in the movie.

The first Jerry Goldsmith soundtrack I bought was *The Secret of NIMH*, still one my favourites, while the first CD I bought was *Explorers* – great music to one of the dodgiest movies I have ever seen. But we all know: The best soundtracks are composed for just average films. It is an astonishing fact that in most blockbusters the music is not as good as the movie.

I started collecting Jerry Goldsmith CDs back then, and in the two years that followed listened predominantly to his music and never getting bored with his genius. Naturally I continued going to his annual concerts in London to listen to the soundtracks and have a chat with other film music enthusiasts.

I was not alone in feeling emotionally empty after Jerry Goldsmith's death in 2004 and film music has never been the same since. I am still looking for a composer to be as passionate about as I was about him, and have yet to find one. I am now following Hans Zimmer, but he is not as gifted as Jerry. Unfortunately, James Horner also died recently, so Patrick Doyle is one of my favourite composers at the moment.

I recently discovered Michael Giacchino and have to say that he is one of today's most talented film music composers. Attending his 50th birthday concert at the Royal Albert Hall in London on 20 October 2017 was one of the most enjoyable film music concert experiences I have ever had. Although I will not be talking about James Newton Howard in this book, his concert *Three Decades of Music for Hollywood* on 3 November 2017 was a highlight in my musical life. Thank you, James Newton Howard, for being such a great guy!

## My blog on amazing movie music

When I was studying digital marketing in San Francisco in 2014, our professors told us that we should put some content onto the World Wide Web to learn about using digital marketing tools, familiarise ourselves with social media and gain more experience of the digital world. A regularly updated blog might be a good place to start.

So, I gave some thought to what I was passionate about. I started with a travel blog, but I was not satisfied with this idea – there are already plenty of travel blogs around, so why should people read mine? I tried different approaches, but then dropped the whole idea altogether and decided to start a blog about film music. I chose to write in a very personal style and always started with a few lines of introduction about why I was discussing a particular soundtrack that week. After two or three paragraphs about the movie and some background information, I offered some insight into the music and the reasons why I liked a particular track in the score or made recommendations about what people should listen to.

I have not studied music or composing, but I did work in the movie industry for seven years and also dealt with some aspects of music. Even though a good soundtrack should be independent of the movie it was originally composed for, you should always bear in mind that film music is music written for a movie, and not intended for a concert hall. The themes, the musical structure and the composing style are mostly a result of the film's genre, topics and dramaturgical storyline. Therefore, a weakness in the music or the dramaturgical structure of a score is very often the result of the weakness of the film.

Orchestral soundtracks are not equal to classical music by the likes of Beethoven, Mozart or Wagner. Some soundtrack composers such as Bill Conti and James Horner used various classical works from composers like Sergei Prokofiev, Aram Khachaturian, Gustav Holst and Dmitri Shostakovich in a way that is more than just a homage. Other composers like John Williams and Jerry Goldsmith are influenced by composers such as Wagner or Bartok, but do not copy their work, and although they might be influenced by them, their composing style is very different.

The idea for my blog was to write weekly about a soundtrack I recommended readers listen to. They were mostly older soundtracks, not the latest ones because I think that the quality of film music has deteriorated recently. I underestimated the amount of time it would take to write a new review, so after a year I reduced the publishing time to every two weeks and have slowed it down even more these days. However, you will find a recent review on my website regularly and can sign up for updates.

A very important part of my blog is the music itself. I therefore also include music tracks on YouTube. Music does not just involve writing about it; it is about listening to and talking about it and so I added a social forum. If you want to check out my blog, visit www.amazingmoviemusic.com

**About this book – What it is, what it is not and what I am proud of**

The idea for this book came about after a discussion with a friend of mine because she said that she felt a little lost on my website. I included a search function, but with over 80 soundtracks discussed now, it is sometimes difficult to find a particular one. That is a typical issue with blogs and digital media.

So, I decided to go back to the traditional method of publishing and started writing this book. I have chosen 50 soundtracks that occupy a special place in my heart. I recommend buying all of them or at least listening to them, not just because they have a special place in my heart, but because they are great examples of amazing movie music and should be part of every soundtrack collection.

Choices made will always attract criticism. I am sure that plenty of people will not agree with my list and believe I should have talked about other soundtracks, skipped some of them etc. I do not blame anyone for criticising my choices; I encourage you to discuss them! This is precisely one of the intentions behind this book: to get people talking about soundtracks, discussing favourite composers and talking about a specific soundtrack that should be rediscovered.

The 50 soundtracks I have chosen are not the fifty best soundtracks of the world because I did not include a lot of marvellous ones by classic movie music composers such as Franz Waxman, Max Steiner and Miklós Rózsa from the Golden Age of film music. I have included just one from that time: Erich Wolfgang Korngold's *The Adventures of Robin Hood*, the reason for which will be explained later.

I have chosen 50 CDs that are simply 50 great soundtracks; a lot of them are timeless and wonderfully composed and orchestrated. They are great examples of how wonderful film music can be, how timeless amazing movie music is, and how much fun we can have listening to and talking about it. For this book, I have rewritten every review, added more information and changed my style of writing. Publishing on a blog is different from writing a book.

These days everybody talks about Hans Zimmer when they think of film music. Hans Zimmer's success was justified but the dominance of Hans Zimmer and his co-composers was not good for the film music industry because other gifted composers were side-lined for a while.

I like Hans Zimmer's soundtracks and will be discussing a few of them, but one intention of this book was also to show that there is much more to discover and that there are plenty of very gifted film music composers out there. Hans Zimmer is a rock star of the film music scene. I attended two of his concerts on his European concert tour: one in Mannheim in Germany, where Hans Zimmer talked in German in a very personal way – thank you for that! – and one in Wembley Arena with amazing visuals. Listening to *Chevaliers de Sangreal* from *The Da Vinci Code* (2006), in my opinion perhaps the best piece of music Hans Zimmer has ever composed, was one of the best moments of my life.

Another intention of this book is therefore to talk about composers who might not be as popular among non-film music enthusiasts, such as Patrick Doyle, John Scott and in particular Michael J. Lewis. I discovered Michael J. Lewis when I was a teenager and will talk about a funny episode with one of the German television companies I had. I found out Michael J. Lewis's contact details and sent him an email asking if he might be interested in answering some questions for my blog. I was so happy when he agreed and the interview he gave me is included in this book. Michael J. Lewis is a very gifted composer and a gentleman to talk to. It is my intention to recommend him to soundtrack collectors once again.

While I was writing my blog, James Horner died in a plane crash. I have been discussing Horner a lot with my friends recently because he was one of the most gifted composers in the film music business. After his death, I posted a very personal note on my blog and for Jerry Goldsmith's 88th birthday I did the same. Jerry, you are truly missed!

This book is just a small guide to the world of amazing movie music, nothing more, but also nothing less.

So, let's get on with the first one.


# II. THE SCORES

# 1. THE SECRET OF NIMH – MY FIRST JERRY GOLDSMITH SCORE

*The Secret of NIMH* is one of the best soundtracks Jerry Goldsmith ever composed. It was also the first movie featuring Goldsmith's music I saw, and the first soundtrack I ever bought. I therefore chose this soundtrack to kick off my film music blog and also wanted to start my book with it.

## The movie

*The Secret of NIMH* (1982) is an American animation movie directed by Don Bluth, the former Animation Director at Disney. It is based on Robert C. O'Brien's novel *Mrs Frisby and the Rats of NIMH* (1971), which I read after seeing the movie. The style of the movie is very like Disney's classic animation style, but it is sometimes very dark, and I do not think some scenes are suitable for very young children. During the production, the name of the main character has changed to Mrs Brisby because of trademark concerns with Frisbee discs. In 1998 it was followed by a direct-to-video sequel without the involvement of Don Bluth or Jerry Goldsmith.

The movie had a complicated production history, as you can find out about in Wikipedia. Bluth intended to return feature animation to its "golden era", so he focused on strong characters, a good story and experimenting with unusual and more labour-intensive animation techniques. Among these techniques were rotoscoping and multiple passes on the camera to achieve transparent shadows and multiple colour palettes for characters to fit in situations with different light. The tight budget resulted in a very tight schedule. Producer Gary Goldman recalled working 110-hour weeks during the final six months. Bluth made several changes to the story, mostly by adding mystical elements that are most apparent in the magic amulet given to Mrs Brisby and the scene in which she uses it.

The film was a financial success. In competition with blockbusters such as Steven Spielberg's *E.T.*, it performed better when it opened than *Poltergeist* (with another great score by Jerry Goldsmith), *Rocky III* (a fabulous Bill Conti score) or *Star Trek II: The Wrath of Khan* (James Horner's best Star Trek score). Compare these with today's scores, and you realise how spoiled we were back then. Owing to the strong competition, *The Secret of NIMH* made just $14 million in North America, but was more successful on home video.

## The music

*The Secret of NIMH* was Jerry Goldsmith's first animation movie, as he explained in the liner notes to the soundtrack release. Goldsmith finally decided to treat this movie as a live action movie and developed the same kind of extended themes and musical structure. He pointed out: "Since *The Secret of NIMH* is the first animated film I've scored, I was initially concerned as to whether the exceptional techniques which animation requires should be reflected in a different approach to the music. After all, animated films in general [...] seek to convincingly create a total environment; everything from the characters' personalities to the clouds in the sky is an "abstract creation", and these elements must convincingly mesh to portray a believable fantasy world."[1]

Goldsmith further explained that scenes are much shorter for animated films than for "live action", and "thus, on reflection, seem to lend themselves to music's playing an even larger, unifying role than usual. I therefore decided to score the picture as though it were live action, believing that this would strengthen the sense of continuity and heighten the feeling of "reality". The first playback with film and sound "in sync" more than convinced me of the correctness of this approach."[2] You can see in the final confrontation between the goodie and the baddie what Goldsmith meant and how right this approach was.

It is very interesting that composing music for animation movies seems to be a very difficult field, and even a very gifted composer such as Elmer Bernstein had trouble finding the right approach in composing the music for Disney's *The Black Cauldron* (1985). Goldsmith returned to animation with his excellent score for Disney's *Mulan* (1998), for which he did not win an Academy Award. Surprisingly, a lot of Disney movies in the 1990s won the Academy Award for best music score, such as long-time winner Alan Menken for *The Little Mermaid* (1989), *Beauty and the Beast* (1991), *Aladdin* (1992) and *Pocahontas* (1995), and even Hans Zimmer for *The Lion King* (1995), but Jerry Goldsmith's score for Disney's *Mulan* did not win an Academy Award, but it was nominated.

Jerry Goldsmith's approach to treating *The Secret of NIMH* like a live action movie was exactly the right one. By doing this, Goldsmith could avoid the typical Mickey Mousing technique. This technique syncs the accompanying music with the action on screen and matches the music to the movement on screen. In early Walt Disney films, the music almost completely works to mimic the animated motions of the characters, as can be seen in the classic Mickey Mouse animation *Steamboat Willie* (1928), the first Mickey Mouse cartoon by Walt Disney, with music by Carl Stalling. However, it was not only animation composers who used Mickey Mousing; Max Steiner uses this technique for the classic *King Kong* (1933).

*The Secret of NIMH* is a very good balanced score between the darker and lighter parts. Therefore, and because Goldsmith is very closely following the dramaturgical structure of the scenes, we have tracks with comedy elements and tracks that are darker because they concentrate on the mystical parts of the story. A good example is the *Main Title*. The film starts with Nicodemus, the wise and mystical leader, telling the story of Mrs Brisby's husband, how he died and what Nicodemus is expecting in the following weeks and months. The score starts with haunting music before the orchestra erupts into the beautiful main theme, played firstly on a trumpet.

Even some tracks are balanced between comedy and action. *Allergic Reaction/Athletic Type* is initially a darker track with some nice action music, and then Goldsmith uses the full force of the orchestra to finish it with a beautiful melody. *The Tractor* is an excellent action track for a very dramatic scene in the movie. Because Mrs Brisby's son Timothy has fallen ill and should stay in bed, Mrs Brisby tries to prevent the farmer from ploughing his field.

I have two favourite tracks. The first is *Moving Day*. This piece is an excellent example of how a composer can build up tension and drama with the music for a scene. The music follows the scene in great detail and has an excellent dramaturgical structure by using different themes. It is modern in a very good way without being atonal, and timeless in its way of being a perfect example of amazing movie music.

Another astonishing track is *Step Into My House*. This music underscores the scene when Mrs Brisby visits Nicodemus. Goldsmith creates a haunting and subsequently magical atmosphere, pure musical magic. Another example of this mystical music is the track called *House Raising*: here Goldsmith composed a fabulous action track for the dramatic showdown when all the animals together try to rescue Mrs Brisby's house, but ultimately fail in. Then Mrs Brisby uses the magic amulet and… but you should see this scene in the movie for yourself. This is excellent musical storytelling!

My second favourite track is the last one called *Flying High/End Titles*. Here Goldsmith gives the film a beautiful ending by musically visualising the final love scene between two ravens, bringing one of his most beautiful love themes to an end. The track is very short but also dangerous in a particular way. Years ago, I was sitting in my apartment in Munich. My idea was just to drink one glass of wine after a long day at work and listen to this track once. In the end, I finished nearly half of the bottle, played the role of the conductor in front of an invisible orchestra, and listened to this track over ten times. The music from 1'21 in particular is excellent.

If you ever start your collection of film music with one soundtrack, I highly recommend starting with this one! This is film music at its highest level of excellence!

## 2.   THE FURY – THE BEST NEVER COMPOSED BERNARD HERRMANN SCORE

John Williams is one of the best well-known composers of film music. Even people who are not fans of soundtracks in general know that John Williams is the composer of the music for *Star Wars* and *Indiana Jones*. Perhaps they also know that Williams composed the music for *Jaws* and *Schindler's List*. The collaboration between John Williams and Steven Spielberg was and is still very successful, and therefore Williams has been able to compose music for very different genres and various movies. His reputation for composing beautiful themes and timeless orchestral soundtracks has led to his involvement with a lot of very talented directors during his career. With *Harry Potter*, Williams got involved with another highly successful franchise, composing the music for the first three *Harry Potter* movies before Patrick Doyle composed the music for the next one, and then Alexandre Desplat took over.

For the first review of a John Williams score in my book, I did not want to choose one of his very popular scores such as *Star Wars*, *Indiana Jones*, *Jaws*, *Home Alone*, *Schindler's List* or *Harry Potter*. Even though these famous scores are great soundtracks, I think that John Williams had his best time in the 1970s with darker scores such as *Dracula* (1979) and *The Fury* (1978), which I will now discuss.

**The movie**

Brian De Palma is a strange director. He has such a talent for visual storytelling, but is often so obsessed with sex and violence that he also is the director of a lot of mediocre movies. *The Fury* is a typical De Palma movie: it has great scenes that you will never forget, but overall the film is not a masterpiece, just half of a good movie.

*The Fury* is a typical 1970s movie when a lot of para-psychological movies were produced, and it was De Palma's next movie after *Carrie* (1976), the excellent adaptation of Stephen King's novel. The idea of psychological war using synthetic drugs to influence people was already discussed in the 1950s. The internet is full of articles about the CIA Project MKUltra, a mind control programme with experiments on humans. The intention was to develop drugs and procedures for use in interrogations and torture to weaken the individual and finally force confessions through mind control. Initially started in the 1950s and officially halted in 1973, MKUltra used numerous methodologies to manipulate people's mental states and alter brain functions, including using drugs such as LSD or hypnosis, sensory deprivation, isolation and other forms of psychological torture.

*The Fury*, based on these ideas, is a weird mixture of mystic elements, horror, SF and romance. Steven Spielberg's first wife, Amy Irving, played perfectly the innocent young woman Gillian who is struggling with forces she cannot control. Kirk Douglas, looking for his son Robin, gives another excellent performance in his later career, along with John Cassavetes as a personification of the devilish US government. The plot is over-complicated with its various subplots and not very politically correct for today's viewing habits but, as always in a De Palma movie, it has some scenes that you will never forget. Two of them are Gillian's escape and the famous last scene.

*The Fury* was one of the first De Palma movies I watched, and I was immediately caught by his way of visual storytelling. Plenty of critics did not like the movie and reacted with confusion. Interesting to mention is here that the famous critic Pauline Kael praised the visual poetry of *The Fury* as being so strong that the weak narrative does not matter.

Even though I later watched a lot of mediocre De Palma movies, in my opinion he is still one of the best directors of the New Hollywood. With De Palma as director, Sean Connery won his only Academy Award for this astonishing performance as Jimmy Malone in *The Untouchables* (1987) with a fabulous score by the legendary Ennio Morricone. *The Fury* is still worth watching today, and even though some scenes now seem trashy to watch, the best reason to put this movie in your DVD player again is John Williams's fantastic music.

## The music

De Palma has always acknowledged the importance of a good music score. Unfortunately, Bernard Herrmann, with whom the director worked on *Sisters* (1973) and *Obsession* (1976) died in December 1975, just after completing the recording of the music for Martin Scorsese's *Taxi Driver*. Therefore, De

Palma hired John Williams to compose a score in Herrmann's style. Similar in style is John Williams's score to John Badham's *Dracula* with Frank Langella as Dracula and Laurence Olivier as Van Helsing.

Years ago, I bought the Varese edition with ten tracks and recently discovered that La-La Land Records produced an expanded version with 32 tracks. This two-CD set offers the music as recorded for the film first and then the soundtrack album from 1978 for which Williams re-recorded the music in London with the London Symphony Orchestra, his favourite orchestra to record music with. Jerry Goldsmith took a similar approach, using the National Philharmonic Orchestra for a lot of recordings of his soundtracks. For this second recording, Williams took a more symphonic approach by combining several cues. He even added the strings-only track entitled *Epilogue*, which reveals the close connection between *The Fury* and Bernard Herrmann's famous *Psycho* score.

*The Main Title*, the first highlight of the score, introduces the haunting main theme that is composed like a valse macabre. This dark music gives a perfect idea of what kind of scary movie that will now be seen. Like in *The Omen* there is no action happening during *The Main Title*, just the credits are shown. It is unfortunate that only a few directors these days use the power of a substantially composed main title to prepare the audience for what is coming.

Owing to its scary aspects, overall *The Fury* is a very dark score. There are some lighter moments, for example the typical Williams scherzo style in *For Gillian* or the lovely *The Search for Robin*, but the best parts of the score are its darker moments. The La-La Land CD brings us some shorter tracks such as *Out of The Water* (after Robin's kidnapping), *The Train Wreck* (with some typical SF music), *Thru the Alley* (which is reminiscent of the *Star Wars* music), *Hester Eavesdropping*, *TV Surveillance*, *The Conspiracy* (with a lovely strings part), *Before Dinner* and *The Fall*, but I prefer the longer tracks of the score. In *Hester's Theme & The House*, we have a kind of love theme that Williams uses for the few quieter moments of the movie when Kirk Douglas is spending time with his girlfriend, Hester. The woodwind sections here are very nicely played. Another more lyrical track is *Coming Down the Stairs*, in which you can hear how powerful the main theme is even in a non-action track. Again, the woodwinds are reminiscent of the Bernard Herrmann's style of composing.

The second highlight after the *Main Title* is *Vision on the Stairs*, a perfect example of musical storytelling. This scene gives you an idea of just how talented De Palma is in telling a story without any dialogue by just focusing on the visual aspects. Gillian who is unable to control her psychic powers, such as telekinesis and extra-sensory perception, has agreed to move into the Paragon Institute to learn more about her skills. When she touches the hand of Charles Durning, the head of the institute, she sees what happened to Robin in a vision. Williams's astonishing music captures the shocking vision and is an excellent example of haunting musical imagination. The version of the original score can be compared with the more symphonic one on the second CD.

The third highlight is *Gillian's Escape*. For me, this scene is the best of the movie and something like the real climax. To finally meet Ex-CIA Agent Peter Sandza, played by Douglas, Gillian escapes from the institute, but is involved in a tragic situation. To increase the suspense and the dramatic content of a scene, De Palma likes to use slow motion for action scenes. Therefore, a scene that would normally last one or two minutes is extended to nearly six minutes. As the music drives this scene forward, the audience does not feel bothered by the use of slow motion.

This six-minute track, perhaps one of the best tracks Williams ever composed, contains all the scene's emotions carried away in the music. Since there is no dialogue in the whole scene, it works like a short silent movie and the effect of the visuals combined with the music is astonishing. Williams uses the lyrical theme when Gillian is finally running on the street, then the combination of strings and brass to build up the suspense and finally melodramatic music when the tragic death occurs.

After this dramatic climax, the movie and the music slow down. The suspense starts again with *Approaching the House*. *Lifting Susan* is another reason to buy the La-La Land CD, another very fine suspense and action track for another shocking scene in the movie. There are four versions of *Death on The Carousel* on the La-La Land CD, and the reason for this is given in the liner notes. *Gillian's Power* underscores the scene with one of the most amazing death scenes in movie history. I am not a big fan of the typical 1970s synth-music on this track, but the final seconds are the perfect music to end this shocking scene, which also closes the movie.

The fourth and last highlight of the score is the track called *Epilogue*, which I mentioned before. Since this is also a track with just strings, people like to compare it with *Psycho*, but this is not fair and was not Williams's intention. His approach is different because this track is not meant to be scary like Herrmann's music for the shocking murder scene in *Psycho*; it is more like a musical coda that brings the album to an end.

*The Fury* is not only one of the best scores for a horror thriller, but one of the most elegant ones as well. Compared to *Dracula*, it lacks a real love theme, but with its dark and gothic horror music, it is highly advanced compared to later horror music in the style of John Carpenter's synthesiser music for *Halloween* (1978). Whether or not *The Fury* is John Williams's best score is not the most critical question to answer. Without a doubt it is amazing movie music and one of the best scores ever written!

# 3. NORTH AND SOUTH – A MODERN GONE WITH THE WIND

Bill Conti is one of my favourite composers. He is mostly known for his music for the *Rocky* (1976) franchise, but Conti has so much more to offer. Perhaps because of his Italian origin, he has a great ability to compose lovely melodies and very dramatic music that emphasises the emotions of a scene. Bill Conti composed the soundtracks for many of Sylvester Stallone's movies such as *F.I.S.T.* (1978), *Paradise Alley* (1978), *Escape to Victory* (1981) and *Lock up* (1989), but also for famous television series such as *Dynasty, The Colbys, Falcon Crest* and *Cagney and Lacey.* Furthermore, Conti composed the music for the *Karate Kid* (1984 to 1994) franchise, the American version of Luc Besson's *The Big Blue* (1988) and the James Bond movie *For Your Eyes Only* (1981).

In the last few years, music companies seem to realise that a lot of soundtracks by Conti were not released, so eventually we got *North and South, Escape to Victory, The Karate Kid* and more. However, I have one wish here: please give us a good edition of *The Thomas Crown Affair* (1999), the smooth music for the remake starring Pierce Brosnan and Rene Russo.

## The series

*North and South* is the title of three American television miniseries broadcast on ABC in 1985, 1986 and 1994. The first two miniseries can be considered as classics, but the third and final instalment is not worth talking about. The first one is still the seventh-highest rated miniseries in TV history and made Patrick Swayze a star.

Producer David Wolper, a long-time independent producer of high-quality documentaries for television, revolutionised TV in 1977 with his award-winning production of Alex Haley's family saga *Roots* about American slavery. In 1983, he produced the classic *The Thorn Birds* with Richard Chamberlain as priest Ralph de Bricassart and Rachel Ward as Meggie, with a fabulous score by Henry Mancini.

*North and South* had two crucial elements for a successful miniseries: a very well-written best-selling novel by John Jakes and a historical subject that is still affecting American life. The plot is about the friendship between Orry Main from South Carolina, played by Swayze, and George Hazard from Pennsylvania, played by James Read, who become best friends while attending the United States Military Academy at West Point. The slave-owning Mains are rural planters, while the Hazards are part of the industrial revolution in the more progressive northern states of the US. The different lifestyles result in conflicts, mainly driven by George's sister Virgilia, played by Kirstie Alley, and her opinion about freedom for the slaves. Orry falls in love with Madeline, played by the beautiful Lesley-Anne Down, but she marries the sadistic Justin LaMotte, played by David Carradine.

The main difference with John Jakes's book is that Orry died in the first book, but in the TV series Orry he survived. Since Swayze was not interested in returning to his role for the third season, he had to be killed at the start. Philip Casnoff as Elkanah Bent, the nemesis of Orry and George, achieves this in the first minutes of the third series. It is clear that the producers used old material for the only scene when you see Orry; the person getting killed is being played by a faceless actor. That was the moment I switched off my TV and did not carry on watching the third series.

Set before and during the American Civil War, the series is a modern *Gone with the Wind* and takes back to those days. The series features a lot of popular and well-known actors such as David Carradine as Madeline's sadistic husband, Hal Holbrook as Abraham Lincoln, Gene Kelly as Bent's father, Robert Mitchum as Colonel Patrick Flynn, Jean Simmons as Orry's mother and Jonathan Frakes as George's older brother, to mention just a few.

Even today, the series is worth watching, and in my opinion Swayze did not get enough credit for his role, even though he sometimes overacted. The action scenes are very good overall, but the second instalment focused perhaps a little bit too much on the sadistic scenes of war. However *North and South* is still great entertainment. Bill Conti did a marvellous job, and his music is one reason that the series become a huge success. As the music of *North and South* is typical of Conti's style of composing, I decided to introduce this composer with this music.

**The music**

After composing the music for the *Rocky* movies, winning an Academy

Award for *The Right Stuff* (1983) and even composing the music for one James Bond movie, Conti was in high demand. Even though he had never scored a mini-series before, Conti already had experience with composing music for television and created the title themes for various successful TV series. In the liner notes to the CD release of *North and South*, Conti explained that producer David Wolper said: "I want *Gone With the Wind*"[3]. After playing the theme on the piano, Wolper and director Richard T. Heffron were very pleased.

In the liner notes, you also get an idea of Conti's great sense of humour when he asked: "When do we go on air?" and got the reply: "In three weeks". He felt that this shortened his life by six months. Conti explained in the liner notes the murderous schedule he was facing, but when listening to the music, you will understand it was worth all the effort. Conti explained that *North and South* is for him "melodic, operatic, Italian", and this approach was 100% right.

"The real miracle is that it happened at all – and that it didn't kill me. I had to write like an animal."[4] For the first week, he composed from early morning until late at night, during the last two weeks, he woke up at six in the morning and wrote until six at night, then went over to the scoring stage and recorded every night from seven to twelve, and this had to start all over again the next day. Conti explained that because of the murderous schedule he was writing in a stream of consciousness, and for Conti as an Italian, that is melodic, operatic, Italian. "I can do that in my sleep, that's me,"[5] he pointed out.

The soundtrack for the series comes in two CD sets called books, each one with three CDs, and the first book also has a fourth CD with source music from this era. The music has a lot of highlights and starts, of course, with the powerful and majestic main theme. There is also a shorter, faster version played for the end credits, and different versions of these main themes can be found throughout the second book.

The tracks for the second book are generally shorter, so it is difficult to highlight a few tracks. It might also be a little boring to listen to the whole music all at once. The music is a little repetitive, but if you consider that the music was over four hours long, that is not surprising. People who know the series can go directly to their favourite scenes and play the music to these scenes.  By listening to the whole soundtrack, you can discover some unexpected highlights such as *Charles Chase* (Disc 1, track 25). People who are familiar with Conti's music will also discover that some parts are very similar to his score to *The Formula* (1981), especially the music for Billy and his love interest Augusta.

In his musical approach, Conti used Richard Wagner's leitmotiv approach, so he used typical themes for each character. Except for the main theme, there are individual themes for the peaceful life in the southern states at that time, an Irish theme for George's wife Constance (Disc 1, track 38), or a heavily percussion-based version of the main theme for the Hazards from the industrial northern states in track 16 *Hazard Iron*.

Because *North and South* is a love story, there are plenty of romantic moments in this fabulous score. One great piece is the love scene between Orry and Madeleine in *Madeline and Orry* (CD 2, track 4), a true masterpiece in the tradition of the melodramatic Italian opera style of Giacomo Puccini. This track alone is worth buying the CD set for. Many of these very emotional and melodramatic pieces can be found in the soundtrack, for example *The Wedding Night*, with a very sad variation on the main theme, or *Church Meeting*, a similar track when Orry sees Madeline at the end of episode 2 as they try to accept their situation as it is right now. How Conti guides the emotions during this scene is indeed a sign of how gifted this composer is.

There are plenty of marvellous action tracks to discover. One is *En Garde, Bent* (CD 1, track 11) when Bent wants to give a sabre lesson to Orry, but Orry is stronger than he expected. Another great track is *Billy's Duel* (CD 3, track 18) about a perilous trap set for Billy and, of course, the full number of action tracks in the second CD set. One track worth mentioning is George's rescue with Orry and Charles in *Orry Frees George* (CD 3, track 04) or a short one called *Charles Chase* (CD 1, track 7), great, fast-forward action music. One highlight is, of course, *Orry to the Rescue* (CD 1, track 24) when Orry finally kills Justin and gets Madeline. This whole track is composed in a scherzo style, a style in which John Williams likes to compose, but overall still pure Conti.

It is practically impossible to mention all the highlights. You have to discover them for yourself, and this is great fun. As someone who watched *North and South* as a teenager and always wanted to have Bill Conti's whole soundtrack in my hands, a dream came true when these two CD sets were finally released. I still prefer the music to the first book, too much war music for me in the second book, but I do not want to miss tracks such as *The Wedding*, when Orry gets finally married to Madeline, or *Augusta Inside*, for the love scenes between Charles and the lovely Augusta. Take your time to discover this music and bring your first listening session to an end with *Friends Farewell* and the shorter version of the main theme at the end.

Bill Conti said in the liner notes: "*North and South* was a great experience. It's one of the things I'm most proud of". I agree. *North and South* is a perfect example of what amazing movie music can do. Well done, maestro!

# 4. ALIENS – VIETNAM IN OUTER SPACE

When thinking of how to introduce James Horner here, I quickly decided to write about *Aliens*. This soundtrack was not the first soundtrack by James Horner I had heard; that was *Willow* (1988), a fabulous score that greatly impressed me with its orchestral power in the action tracks and the lovely main theme. But even though I like *Willow* very much and think it is one of the best soundtracks by James Horner, I will not discuss this score in my book. I want to talk about *Aliens* because it is one of the most popular and important soundtracks in James Horner's career.

I was so lucky to see the movie at the Royal Albert Hall in London on 6 November 2016 with a live performance by the Royal Philharmonic Concert Orchestra conducted by Ludwig Wicki and an enthusiastic audience of 7,500 people. James Horner and London had a special relationship because the composer attended the prestigious Royal College of Music. Horner's initial ambition was to compose avant-garde classical music, and therefore he spent a year studying under the renowned composer György Ligeti in Hamburg before finishing his academic studies back in native California. He then realised that writing music for concert halls might be a dead end, so he switched to the film music genre.

Like James Cameron, James Horner was part of the Roger Corman troupe and was assigned to one low-budget SF movie called *Battle Beyond The Stars* (1980). This movie is long forgotten, but because of James Horner's music still worth seeing. You can buy a CD with the soundtrack and will then discover a lot of the typical and now famous James Horner sound.

As a special surprise after the live performance of *Aliens*, James Cameron, Sigourney Weaver and Gale Ann Hurd came on stage and showed their respect to James Horner who died on 22 June 2015 in a plane crash. I was living in San Francisco and working for Google in Mountain View at that time and was shocked when I checked my phone after leaving the office and read the sad news about Horner's death.

James Horner was without any doubt one of the most talented film music composers ever. With his sense of drama, his ability to use the full force of the orchestra, his talent for writing lovely melodies and his fruitful collaboration with directors such as James Cameron, Mel Gibson, Martin Campbell and Ron Howard, he was able to compose the music for some great blockbusters. The Academy Award for *Titanic* was finally highly deserved, even though I think that this score is really not one of Horner's best soundtracks.

*Aliens* is far better music and also a fine example for the close connection between classical music and Horner's soundtrack. Horner liked to use motifs or themes from classical pieces, especially from Sergei Prokofiev's *Romeo and Juliet* (listen, for example, to the beginning of the track *Stealing The Enterprise* from *Star Trek III: The Search for Spock* (1984)) or for *Aliens*, the adagio from the first ballet suite *Gayaneh* (1942) composed by the Soviet Armenian Aram Khachaturian. Later in his career, Horner also composed soundtracks that sound very similar to earlier ones, so it is possible to speak of a James Horner sound or, if you want to be mean, you can call it self-plagiarism.

Horner's death in a single-fatality crash with his own turboprop aircraft was a shock. He is missed, but I hope people will not just remember him as the composer of *Titanic* and the famous Celine Dion song. Among Horner's contribution to the animation genre are great scores such as *An American Trail* (which I will discuss in my book, too), *The Land before Time* (1988) and *Balto* (1995). Check these out! I will be discussing one of Horner's best scores, the music for *Star Trek II: The Wrath of Khan* (1982) later in this book.

## The movie

*Aliens* is a 1986 American SF/action/horror film written and directed by James Cameron, produced by Gale Anne Hurd and starring Sigourney Weaver, Carrie Henn, Michael Biehn, Lance Henriksen and Bill Paxton. It is the sequel to the 1979 classic *Alien*, directed by Ridley Scott with a fabulous score by Jerry Goldsmith. *Alien* is considered a ground-breaking movie in a lot of ways, one of which was introducing Swiss sculptor and painter H.R. Giger to the movie business. *Aliens* follows Ellen Ripley as she returns to the moon where her crew encountered the hostile Alien creature, this time accompanied by a unit of space marines.

Cameron wrote a 45-page treatment for this *Alien* sequel before he started shooting *Terminator* (1984) which made Arnold Schwarzenegger a star. The producers liked the ideas, so Cameron was also appointed director. This movie was heavily action-packed, and the audience was finally able to see not only one Alien, they see a lot of them, and these Aliens are ready and very willing to kill. Some critics say this movie was like Vietnam in space. Cameron was given a budget of $18 million, and the film grossed $180 million worldwide.

In an interview with Richard Schickel in *Time*, Cameron pointed out he was inspired by the situation in the Vietnam war: a lot of soldiers with modest equipment find out that their weapons and their training are inappropriate for the situation they are facing. Therefore, *Aliens* can be described as War in Space or as a "Vietnam allegory on another planet." [6]

## The music

It was the second time that James Horner composed the music to a sequel. With *Star Trek II*, he established himself as a mainstream composer. Director Nicholas Meyer said that he hired Horner for this movie because he could not afford Jerry Goldsmith, but years later when Meyer directed the sixth *Star Trek* movie, he could no longer afford to hire James Horner.

Cameron knew Horner from their time with Roger Corman, and the director wanted a different score for the sequel of *Alien*. The music should emphasise the action scenes and military aspects of the movie. Cameron put a lot of pressure on Horner and gave him just two weeks to compose the score.

Horner complained about Cameron's behaviour and was exhausted after the recording sessions.

In the liner notes, you can read that almost every cue was tracked and re-edited in the final releases: "Virtually no cue, save for the Main and End Titles, are where they should be, and no cue (except for *Bishop's Countdown*) plays in its entirety as it was written."[7] Nick Redman did a tremendous job in his notes to the Deluxe Edition of the score to give an insight how the music was used in the final cut of the movie. Cameron also used two cues from the original *Alien* score by Jerry Goldsmith (*Sleepy Alien* and *Parker's Death*). Based on the experience on *Aliens*, it took Horner and Cameron eleven years to work together again, this time on *Titanic*, and both received Academy Awards for their second collaboration. *Aliens* received seven Academy Award nominations, one for the score, and one for Sigourney Weaver, the first time that a best actress had been awarded for an action, horror or SF movie.

*Aliens* is a great action score with fresh new ideas; the use of percussion in particular is remarkable. The London Symphony Orchestra played, conducted by Horner who was very happy with the orchestra's performance and his experience with recording a score in London as he had before with *Project Brainstorm* in 1983. The Deluxe Edition features 75 min of music. It has a lot of tracks that were not used in the final movie because Horner was forced to compose the music without seeing the finished movie. Cameron was still directing and behind the film's deadline.

If you do not have this score in your collection, I highly recommend buying it, especially the "Deluxe Edition". The liner notes are very helpful, and there are a lot of additional tracks on the album that are worth hearing. Take the chance to listen to the additional *Ripley's Rescue* track with just the percussion section. Horner was great in composing fast-forward action tracks such as *Futile Escape* and *Ripley's Rescue*. He had a great sense of drama and was highly praised for developing melodies and creating emotions with this music. Horner's usage of the melody from *Gayaneh* is a beautiful musical expression of how lonely it must feel in space.

Wikipedia reports that some tracks from the soundtrack have been used many times in trailers for other movies. As of April 2011, there were reportedly 24 different movie trailers that used *Bishop's Countdown* alone. James Horner composed very many great soundtracks in his career, but in my opinion *Aliens* is by far one of his best. After seeing it live on stage, I have to say that Horner cannot be praised highly enough for this soundtrack.

# 5. Mary Shelley's Frankenstein – Larger than Life in Every Way

I discovered Patrick Doyle when I was still in school with his score to the romantic thriller *Dead Again* (1991), a movie I had not seen before. I was immediately entranced by its powerful orchestration, the dynamic main theme and the beauty of the love theme in this score. To introduce Patrick Doyle in his book, I decided to start with his music for *Mary Shelley's Frankenstein* (1994), a score that is very typical for Doyle and one I highly recommend buying.

When my favourite film music composer, Jerry Goldsmith, died and I was tired of listening to Hans Zimmer, I became a big fan of Doyle's music and watched, for example, *Henry V* (1989), *Needful Things* (1993), *Much Ado About Nothing* (1993), *Great Expectations* (1998), *Killing Me Softly* (2002), *Nanny McPhee* (2005), *The Last Legion* (2207), *Nim's Island* (2008), *Thor* (2011), *Rise of the Planet of the Apes* (2011), *Jack Ryan: Shadow Recruit* (2014) and *Cinderella* (2015) just because Doyle composed the music and, for some of them, because Kenneth Branagh was the director. Patrick Doyle is one of the few composers whose soundtrack I buy without even seeing the movie beforehand, and a few of his scores are among my favourites in my collection. The track *Art and The Minister* from *Needful Things* is the track that holds the record of my most listened-to track ever.

## The movie

I was always a big fan of the Frankenstein movies and read the book when I was a teenager. Kenneth Branagh established himself as a director who was not only able to bring entertaining Shakespeare adaptions such as *Henry V.* or *Much Ado About Nothing* to the big screen, but also directed suspense thrillers such as *Dead Again*. So, I was really excited to see these two very gifted people working together on a Frankenstein movie. This was a must-see for me!

Most critics think that *Mary Shelley's Frankenstein* is not a great movie. It has good scenes, but overall the movie is so over the top in a lot of aspects with too much pathos, too many scenes with Branagh showing his very well-trained body, too much violence and too much Shakespeare-style drama in the dialogue.

These might all be true, but overall *Mary Shelley's Frankenstein* is a very entertaining movie with many scenes that you will remember after seeing it and still one of the best adaptations of Mary Shelley's famous novel. Robert De Niro gave a good performance, but the critics were also right that some scenes were not very convincing.

When I read the book as a teenager, the cover warned me that this is not a book for a young boy, and that is true. The novel has a complicated structure, consists mostly of letters written between Arctic Explorer Captain Robert Walton and his sister. Branagh is the only director who starts his movie with this frame story and shows the final scene of the book set close to the North Pole, a powerful ending to the film. Considering that Shelley was just 18 years old when she wrote the book, *Frankenstein or The Modern Prometheus* is a fabulous novel. The book was inspired by many elements from English and German gothic novels and can be considered as the first real science fiction story.

When you read the novel for the first time and have seen most of the Frankenstein movies before, you really cannot understand why not just one director has tried to adapt it as close to the book as possible. Hammer's *Frankenstein* movies with Peter Cushing are real classics, especially the first two, but to be honest, sometimes the plots are fairly weak and without Cushing's acting no one would watch these movies today.

Kenneth Branagh was the first to take the novel by its heart. His *Frankenstein* features astonishing scenes, e.g. the creation of the monster or the showdown (a new ending compared to the book), but overall Branagh was also unable to create a very convincing movie. Even though De Niro gave a very good performance, one of the greatest weaknesses of the movie is the monster. It is just too scary in its appearance.

In the novel, the creature is described very vaguely: it is ugly, with translucent yellowish skin pulled so taut over the body that it barely disguises the workings of the arteries and muscles underneath; it has watery, glowing eyes, flowing black hair, black lips and white teeth. Boris Karloff acting as the creature was so successful that people still have his performance in mind when thinking of Frankenstein's creature, and James Whale's two *Frankenstein* movies are horror classics.

Although Branagh's movie reminds you sometimes of a Shakespeare drama, with its high focus on tragedy and melancholic dialogue scenes, his adaptation is still one of the best. Unfortunately, there are some very rough violent scenes that are unnecessary. The showdown with Elizabeth is worth seeing and unforgettable, and combined with Doyle's music a very haunting scene.

## The music

Patrick Doyle's music is without any doubt one of the best parts of this movie. This score was the second CD by Patrick Doyle I bought for my collection, and after listening to it, I finally fell in love with this composer's style of composing.

This soundtrack is Doyle at his best, with all his greatness, but also with weaknesses. Doyle is not as sophisticated as composer as Jerry Goldsmith or John Williams, but he is a great film music composer when you give him a story full of action, passion and romantic moments. His ability to go to the heart of a scene, combined with his sense of drama and his ability to write lovely melodies, increases the emotions of a scene to the full, which is precisely the function of an excellent film music composer.

For *Mary Shelley's Frankenstein* Doyle created a majestic main theme, a lovely romantic theme for the quieter moments and very overblown music, e.g. for the *Creation* scene, which perfectly underscores the emotions, but also increases the over-the-top attitude of the movie. The orchestration of this score, undertaken by Doyle's long-time orchestrator Lawrence Ashmore, focuses heavily on the brass section of the orchestra and gives the movie the power that it sometimes lacks. The score is very dynamic and very loud and should be listened to on full volume to develop its musical power. Despite the brutal force in the action tracks of the score, Doyle created a beautiful love theme that you can hear, for example in *The Wedding Night*.

In the liner notes, Doyle pointed out the concept of the music: "The score for Frankenstein proved to be altogether a "monster" needing a large orchestra to achieve specific orchestral effects in order to match many grand images on screen. Before filming began, Ken asked me to write a melody to the words of Byron's poem "So we'll go no more a roving," as the plan initially was to have a song featured during the ballrooms scene. The idea was eventually discarded but the theme remained. The love theme, featured in its entirety under *The Wedding Night* scene, and all subsequent thematic development stemmed directly from this love melody." [8]

For me, it is astonishing how Doyle can cover the full range of emotions of the movie in his score. As can be seen in his score to Kenneth Branagh's *Cinderella*, he works best with Branagh as director. In the liner notes, Doyle also added some comments about the religious aspects and challenges of the music for the famous creation scene. The film "has numerous religious images with frequent references to God and the immorality of creating life. This was a crucial element and is never more apparent than when Victor is walking away from the monster who hangs suspended like Christ on the Cross from the rafters of Victor's magnificent cathedral-like attic. [...] The creation of The Monster and Elizabeth were two challenging large orchestral moments, whilst other more intimate scenes, such as *She's Beautiful* and *Yes I Speak* called for a smaller orchestral force." [9]

*Mary Shelley's Frankenstein* received mixed reviews, made $22 million in the US and more on the global market. It was a financial success in the end, but not the success people expected. Critic Janet Maslin from *The New York Times* summarised the problems the audience had with this movie, but also showed that she has a total misunderstanding of the novel and the subject of Frankenstein in general: "Unlike Francis Ford Coppola, who is a producer of this film and whose homage to *Dracula* was a more stylish, rapturous undertaking, Mr Branagh is in over his head. He displays neither the technical finesse to handle a big, visually ambitious film nor the insight to develop a stirring new version of this story. Instead, this is a bland, no-fault Frankenstein for the '90s, short on villainy but loaded with the tragically misunderstood. Even the Creature, an aesthetically challenged loner with a father who rejected him, would make a dandy guest on any daytime television talk show." [10] Poor Maslin, she did not understand that this father subject is one of the most important subjects of the novel.

Anyway, enjoy Doyle's score despite what the critics said. I recommend listening to the following tracks and watching the movie if you have not seen it.

Track 1 *To Think of A Story* (beginning)

Track 9 *The Creation* (no comments necessary anymore)

Track 11 *The Escape* (action…)

Track 15 *William* (a very powerful scene in the movie)

Track 16 *Death of Justice*

Track 18 *God Forgive Me* (second creation starts)

Track 19 *Please Wait*

Track 20 *The Honeymoon* (one of the highlights)

Track 21 *The Wedding Night* (the love theme)

Track 23 *She's Beautiful* (showdown music)

Track 24 *He was my father* (the majestic finale that brings the score to a satisfying end)

# 6. North by Northwest – A musical tour de force

The collaboration between director Alfred Hitchcock and composer Bernard Herrmann is perhaps the most successful in movie history. Many directors like to work with the same composer on their movies – think of the collaborations between Paul Verhoeven, Fred Schepisi, Joe Dante and Franklin J. Schaffner with Jerry Goldsmith, Steven Spielberg's friendship with John Williams, Christopher Nolan with Hans Zimmer, John Landis with Elmer Bernstein, Tim Burton with Danny Elfman, Robert Zemeckis with Alan Silvestri, John G. Avildsen with Bill Conti or Kenneth Branagh with Patrick Doyle.

Jerry Goldsmith described the first time a composer meets the director to be like a boy's first date with a girl: both are a little bit shy and have no idea what to expect from each other, and therefore it is quite understandable that if the girl and the boy get along, they want to continue with their collaboration.

In Herrmann, Hitchcock, the master of suspense, found his master of music, and it is a great tragedy that both their egos were ultimately too big to continue working together. Herrmann was not willing to give Hitchcock the pop score the producers of *Torn Curtain* (1966) wanted, and Hitchcock was not willing to continue dealing with Herrmann's complex personality. Their collaboration therefore ended, and in my opinion the best period in Hitchcock's career as well.

I discovered Bernard Herrmann as a teenager when I started watching Hitchcock movies. I was immediately carried away by the unusual orchestration of the action tracks and the composer's ability to create beautiful love music and dynamic action tracks. It can be argued whether I should have introduced Bernard Herrmann with his more famous score to *Psycho*, but in my opinion *North by Northwest* is a score with more variety and therefore is more characteristic of this composer.

### The movie

Alfred Hitchcock created with *North by Northwest* his ultimate thriller, using the main story of a case of mistaken identity. This movie is perfectly balanced between action, romance and comedy. It is interesting that after this movie Hitchcock directed *Psycho*, a movie that is the opposite in its storytelling and one of the first slasher movies. Without *Psycho*, John Carpenter's *Halloween* would never have been possible. I will be discussing *Psycho* later in this book.

*North by Northwest* screenwriter Ernest Lehman, who also wrote the screenplay to Hitchcock's last movie *Family Plot*, wanted to write the "Hitchcock picture to end all Hitchcock pictures". If you compare *North by Northwest* with *Psycho*, I think he achieved his goal.

One explanation for the title might be that it refers to a compass direction that does not exist, so the title may be symptomatic of the whole picture. In the scene when Leo G. Carroll explains to Cary Grant what is the plot all about, Hitchcock put some airplane noise over the scene so that there is no clue why James Mason is hunting Cary Grant all the time. Later in the movie, it says "government secrets" without giving exact information.

There are hundreds of articles written about *North by Northwest*, so it is practically impossible to mention all the interesting facts about it. For me, this movie is timeless and has a few scenes that are astonishing. I am not only referring to the showdown on Mount Rushmore, but I also love the crop duster sequence in particular. Hitchcock's intention was to create a new attack scene that was the opposite of the cliché so far. Therefore, Cary Grant is not attacked at night in a dark street, but instead hunted on a sunny day in an open field.

When I was a young teenager and saw this movie for the first time, I was too innocent to understand the intention of the last scene when the train enters the tunnel. Hitchcock always had trouble with censors, so he chose that kind of scene as an ending. In *North by Northwest*, one of Eva Marie Saint's lines in the dining-car seduction scene had to be redubbed. She originally said, "I never make love on an empty stomach", but it was changed in post-production to "I never discuss love on an empty stomach" because the censors considered the original version too crude. So, what did Hitch do in the last scene, perhaps as a kind of revenge of the constant struggle with censors and the Hays Code: Cary Grant and Eve-Marie Saint are kissing, and you see then a train entering a tunnel at high speed. This is just gorgeous!

**The music**

Bernard Herrmann had previously collaborated with Hitchcock on four movies. For me his best scores for Hitchcock are *North by Northwest*, *Vertigo* and *Psycho*. My favourite is *Vertigo*. For *North by Northwest* Herrmann composed three types of music: chase, suspense and love music. The romantic music has its origins in the typical romantic music of the late nineteenth century.

What Herrmann added to this late nineteenth century style is the large number of percussion instruments. This makes sense because *North by Northwest* is a movie about a chase, and the percussion drives the suspense and the action forward, especially in the showdown. Herrmann used as its basis a fandango, a Spanish couples dance that is usually in triple metre, traditionally accompanied by guitars, castanets or hand-clapping. This energetic track sets the tone for the whole music and the movie. Perhaps the music for the main title is also a musical expression of the chaotic life in New York?

But why this South American rhythm for a movie that takes places in North America? Christopher Husted wrote in the liner notes: "Herrmann referred to Cary Grant's particular "Astaire-like agility" as an inspiration for his use of the Spanish dance called the fandango in the most animated music in the score, typified by the Overture. Because it is a story of a chase, the score is preoccupied with driving, dancing rhythm. The primary character of the Overture is its vigorous, unrelenting cadence – a simple figure chasing heading through the music." [11]

The love theme is one of Herrmann's best, and this lyrical theme is first heard in the train dining sequence. I have to say that I am not a big fan of Eva Maria Saint. I think Grace Kelly was the perfect Hitchcock actress, and that is the reason Hitchcock hired her for three movies. Even after her marriage to Prince Rainier III in April 1956, she was interested in returning to the movie business after a few years because she felt bored in Monaco. She considered playing the female character in *Marnie* (1964) but, of course, Rainier was not happy to see his wife in a role like that and so Gracia Patricia did not accept the role. But imagine Grace Kelly and Sean Connery in this movie together, with Bernard Herrmann's hypnotic and neurotic music. This would have resulted in a far better movie than *Marnie* actually was.

Herrmann's love theme for *North by Northwest* consists of an interplay between the oboe and the clarinet, supported by strings. The rhythm transforms the movement of a train into something musical. Great work, Mr Herrmann! Christopher Husted identified another theme, a third theme, in the score and called it the *Kaplan* theme because Kaplan is the name of the character Cary Grant is considered to be. This theme was borrowed and extended from Herrmann's score for *On Dangerous Ground* (1952)[12], and this theme can be heard expressed most completely in the track called *The Cafeteria*.

For a long time, fans of the score were just able to get it in a version of it conducted by Laurie Johnson, but if you compare this recording with Herrmann's original, you realise how important it is to always buy a score conducted by Herrmann himself.

I want to mention the last tracks for the showdown. Herrmann again used the full power of the orchestra to build suspense, especially in the scene in which Martin Landau comes closer and steps on Grant's hand so that he will fall off the monument. The percussion is perfectly used to increase the suspense in this scene, a highly effective way of getting the audience emotionally involved until the final relief comes when the bad guy is killed.

*North by Northwest* is a classic film music score and just as a good score should be: astonishing in supporting the emotions of the movie, timeless in its musical approach and composing style, and with a main theme that you will never forget once you hear it. Really amazing movie music! It is so regrettable that Hitchcock and Herrmann did not continue their fruitful collaboration for longer.

# 7. EXPLORERS – MY FIRST JERRY GOLDSMITH CD

Jerry Goldsmith's *Explorers* occupies a special place in my heart. It is my one of my favourite Jerry Goldsmith soundtracks, the first soundtrack CD and the second Jerry Goldsmith soundtrack I bought, and the score that made Jerry Goldsmith my favourite composer. Obviously, a pretty important score for me.

## The movie

*Explorers* (1985) is a science fiction family film written by Eric Luke and directed by Joe Dante, who directed classics such as *Gremlins* (1984), *Innerspace* (1987), *The 'Burbs* (1989), *Gremlins 2* (1990), *Matinee* (1993), *Small Soldiers* (1998) and *Looney Tunes: Back in Action (2003)*, for all of which Jerry Goldsmith composed the music, and *Looney Tunes* was his last one.

The film stars Ethan Hawke and River Phoenix in their film debuts – Jason Presson plays the third teenage schoolboy – and this teenage trio builds a spacecraft to explore outer space. The production ran into a great deal of trouble and therefore Dante did not have enough time to finish the movie: "The studio changed hands in the middle of production, and they decided they needed the movie much quicker than we thought," said the director in an interview that can be seen on YouTube. Dante submitted a rough cut, but Paramount wanted to take advantage of the busy summer market: "They said 'just stop editing the picture, we're gonna put it out, and we got a perfect date for it, and we know it'll make a lot of money…", but the movie was a flop.

However, that is not the end of the story. Over the years the movie has gained a cult following and has now a huge fan community. I also watched the film just because I know Joe Dante is its director and Jerry Goldsmith composed the music. Unfortunately, Dante has not been able to produce a director's cut of the movie because apparently the missing scenes are lost. The reason *Explorers* is still popular is also that Jerry Goldsmith composed one of his best scores for it.

## The music

*Explorers* was one of the movies I recorded on tape and filtered the music out – a great deal of work! So, I was one of the happiest people on earth when I discovered there is a soundtrack album available to buy!

*Explorers* really needs another soundtrack release. I will concentrate on the official Varese album that just had nine score tracks. Intrada released a CD with the whole album, over 70 minutes long, but this release is sold out. The Varese album does not start with the main title music, but with *The Construction*, the music for the scene when they build the spacecraft, a highly energetic and fun piece that is a great example of Goldsmith's ability to combine electronics and the traditional sound of the orchestra.

It's hard to believe that this track is now over 30 years old because it still sounds so fresh and enjoyable! Goldsmith brings this track to a beautiful ending with a slow pause before the piece finally concludes. It is still one of my most favourite tracks, especially with the "bouncing" piano at the beginning!

The score is Goldsmith at his best: very entertaining, full of great themes and funny funky arrangements such an in *She Likes Me* for the alien child. Joe Dante asked Goldsmith to compose the music in the Americano style; this composing style can be found in Goldsmith's *Poltergeist* (the first track) but also in the neighbourhood theme for *The Burbs* as a musical narration of typical American neighbourhood life.

Track 3 *No Air* features the space motif and more synthesisers, composed in Goldsmith's typical 80s style, with a main focus on the brass section which was also typical for Goldsmith's music that time.

Track 5 *First Flight* is another highlight in the score. It is interesting to compare the various *First Flight* tracks Goldsmith composed during his career. Think about the wonderful track called *First Flight* for the DDR drama *Night Crossing* (1982), a picture nobody remembers today, or the track *First Flight* in the famous WWI drama *The Blue Max* (1966) starring George Peppard who later became very popular as leader of *The A-Team*.

Track 6 *Free Ride* occasionally reminds me of Goldsmith's score to *The Secret Of NIMH*, with some Micky Mousing here too. Track 7 *Fast Getaway* is an action track, like the action tracks for Joe Dante's *Innerspace* from 1987.

Track 9 *Have A Nice Trip* is the last track of the score, a wonderfully composed piece, eight minutes long, that brings the soundtrack to a fantastic ending. Balancing the orchestra with heavily used electronics, the beautiful main theme can be heard again before we go over to the electronics, and finally, in the last two minutes, the orchestra takes over with the main theme and brings the track to a symphonic ending, the last orchestral track of the album and the final highlight of the score.

*Explorers* is film music at his best: a wonderful score with a great main theme, enjoyable music even without seeing the movie, still fresh in its composing style, and a great example of a musical genius. Truly amazing movie music! We want this score again in a new release please!

# 8. THE ADVENTURES OF ROBIN HOOD – A CLASSIC SCORE

When I was thinking of reviews for this book, I was not sure if I should also include scores from the Classic Age of Hollywood by composers such as Max Steiner, Dimitri Tiomkin, Franz Waxman, Miklós Rózsa and Erich Wolfgang Korngold. Typically, I should have done so because you cannot write a book about film music without including these composers.

On the other hand, however, the idea of this book was not to compete with such astonishing film music books such as Tony Thomas's *Film Score: The Art and Craft of Movie Music* or *Music for the Movies*. If you do not have them in your library, then I highly recommend buying them, especially the second book, because Tony Thomas gives a broad overview of the topic and introduces each composer with plenty of details about their life and their music.

The idea behind my book is not to compete with Tony Thomas because this is nearly impossible – he is such a gifted writer and his knowledge of the topic is impressive. My intention is to provide guidance about the world of film music with 50 scores that are very enjoyable and worth listening to. This does not mean that scores such as Max Steiner's *Gone With The Wind*, Franz Waxman's *Bride Of Frankenstein* or Miklós Rózsa's *Ben Hur* are not enjoyable or not worth buying – I highly recommend buying and listen to them because they are marvellous.

However, I discovered that out of all these classic scores, Erich Wolfgang Korngold's *Robin Hood* is the one I like to listen to most. Even though it was composed in 1938, it still sounds so fresh that I want to discuss this score as the only example in my book from the Golden Age of Hollywood. So, let's start with some basic comments about the composer.

### The composer

Along with Max Steiner and Alfred Newman, Erich Wolfgang Korngold is considered one of the founders of film music. The 1938 Academy Award for his score to *The Adventures of Robin Hood* marked the first time an Oscar was awarded to the composer rather than to the head of the studio music department, as had occurred before for example with Korngold's award-winning score to *Anthony Adverse* in 1936.

Korngold (1897-1957) was born in Moravia, at that time a city in Austria-Hungary but now in the Czech Republic, and owing to his musical talent was considered a "wonder boy". Austrian composer Gustav Mahler called Korngold a "musical genius". At 11, Korngold composed a ballet called *Der Schneemann* (*The Snowman*), wrote his first orchestral score at 14 and his first opera *Die tote Stadt* (*The Dead City*) at 23.

Even Bavarian composer Richard Strauss and the famous Italian composer Giacomo Puccini praised him. The legendary theatre director Max Reinhard brought Korngold to the US, and in 1938 Korngold was asked by Warner Brothers to compose the score for *The Adventures of Robin Hood* starring Errol Flynn. Korngold was Jewish and therefore, he was forced to leave Europe to avoid the Nazi terror. In the liner notes to the CD of *The Adventure of Robin Hood*, Korngold's son George writes about the background story to this music and the struggle his father had composing it.

### The movie

*The Adventures of Robin Hood,* directed by the legendary Michael Curtiz and co-director William Keighley, is not only one of Errol Flynn's best films, but nevertheless I still think it is the best Robin Hood adaptation ever. Even after nearly 80 years, the movie is still fun and has such a great sense of humour. The cast is one of the best, with Olivia de Havilland as Lady Marian, Basil Rathbone as the baddie Guy of Gisbourne and Claude Rains as Prince John.

With a budget of $2 million, this movie was the most expensive film Warner Brothers had ever made, and it was unusually extravagant for the studio that had made a name for itself producing low-budget gangster movies. A funny story is that stuntmen, padded with balsa wood on metal plates, were paid $150 per arrow to be shot by professional archer Howard Hill. Hill was later cast as the man defeated by Robin in the archery tournament. To win, Robin splits the arrow of Philip of Arras, a captain of the guard under Gisbourne. Buster Wiles – a stuntman and close friend of Errol Flynn – maintains that the arrow-splitting stunt was carried out using an extra-large arrow (for the target) and that the second arrow had a wide, flat arrowhead and was fired along a wire.

The movie was a great success, and contemporary views highly positive. *The Adventures of Robin Hood* became the sixth-highest-grossing film of the year, with over $4 million in revenues, at a time when the average ticket price was less than 25 cents. Warner Brothers was so pleased with the results that the studio cast Flynn in two more colour epics before the end of the decade, the western *Dodge City* (1939) and the historical romantic drama *The Private Lives of Elizabeth and Essex* (1939), featuring another score by Erich Wolfgang Korngold.

## The music

Max Reinhardt, the Austrian-born American director and theatrical producer, was very famous for his innovative stage productions and regarded as one of the most prominent directors of German-language theatre in the early 20th century. Reinhardt, with whom Korngold had collaborated on the operetta *Die Fledermaus*, asked the composer to come to Hollywood in 1934 and adapt Felix Mendelssohn's *A Midsummer Night's Dream* for his film version of the play.

In 1938, Korngold was conducting opera in Austria when he was asked by Warner Brothers to return to Hollywood and compose a score for *The Adventures of Robin Hood*. George Korngold explained in the liner notes that his father was busy with composing his fifth and last opera *Die Kathrin*. He agreed and returned by ship, the "worst crossing ever of the great French liner *Normandie*"[13], as George Korngold explains in the liner notes. Overwhelmed by the huge amount of action in this movie, Korngold turned the task down: "I am a musician of the heart, of passions and psychology: I am not a musical illustrator for a 90% action picture."[14]

His plan to return to Vienna was destroyed by Hitler and the Nazis. The Nazis invaded Austria, and the so-called "Anschluss" of Austria took place. Korngold went back to the movie and composing the music but, as his son pointed out, constantly kept complaining during these six hectic weeks of composing that "I just can't do it"[15] throughout the night. On 13 March, Korngold got the news that the Gestapo, Germany's brutal secret police, had occupied the Korngold house in Vienna and confiscated all the Jewish family's belongings. Korngold and his family had to stay in California, with the composer saying later: "We thought of ourselves as Viennese; Hitler made us Jewish."[16]

Korngold treated each film as an "opera without singing"[17] – each character has its own leitmotif in the way that German opera composer Richard Wagner composed the music for his operas. For *The Adventures of Robin Hood* Korngold created an intensely romantic and richly melodic score. For Robin, Korngold composed a sweeping, heroic trumpet theme. As George Korngold pointed out, his father used some music he had composed for classical pieces before, and later used for his classical pieces themes he had composed for the movies.

Even though composing for movies was not Korngold's original intention as a composer, George Korngold explained that his father was excited by the chance to "write music and immediately hear it played by a wonderful orchestra!"[18] For Warner Brothers, Korngold composed the music for 11 movies in the next eight years and liked the movie medium as a new form of art that provided a unique vehicle for dramatic music. George Korngold said that his father later gave up composing music for movies just because the movies he was offered were of "decreasing artistic merit".[19]

*The Adventures of Robin Hood* is definitely the ultimate Korngold score. Korngold's personal favourite was the more mysterious music for *Between Two Worlds* (1944), a film set during World War II featuring John Garfield, Paul Henreid and Eleanor Parker. The richness of the colourful music, the lovely melodies and the terrific action music make *The Adventures of Robin Hood* a perfect example of timeless movie music. It cannot be overestimated how much this score influenced the film music genre. If you listen to John Williams, you know how much he rated Korngold's music and his approach to treating movies as an "opera without singing". Korngold's intention was that, when divorced from the moving image, these scores could stand alone in the concert hall, and it is astonishing how fresh the music still sounds.

Korngold would later say that the film score of *The Adventures of Robin Hood* saved his life. He won the Academy Award for Best Original Score, and was later nominated for *The Private Lives of Elizabeth and Essex* (1939) and *The Sea Hawk* (1940).

**Korngold's fame**

Despite his achievements, for years Korngold attracted almost no positive critical attention. Then, in 1972, RCA Victor released an LP entitled *The Sea Hawk*, Korngold's last score for a swashbuckler film, featuring excerpts from Korngold's scores performed by the National Philharmonic Orchestra conducted by Charles Gerhardt and supervised by George Korngold. This was followed by recordings of Korngold's operas and concert works, which led to performances of his symphony and concertos, as well as other compositions.

In 1943, Korngold became a naturalised citizen of the United States. Two years later, World War II came finally to an end and Korngold was eager to return to writing music for the concert hall. For *Magic Fire* (1956), a biographical film about the life of Richard Wagner, Korngold returned to the movie business, adapted Wagner's music for the movie, wrote some original music and is seen during the final scenes as the conductor Hans Richter. While Korngold's late-Romantic composing style was no longer in demand at the time he died, his score for *The Adventures of Robin Hood* is film music at its best and amazing movie music! By listening to this score, it is clear how much John Williams in his rich 19th-century music style was influenced by Korngold's film music concept. Without Korngold, a John Williams might not have been possible.

# 9. Romancing The Stone – A funky jazz adventure

*Romancing the Stone* (1984) is one of my teenage memories and, in my opinion, the score to this movie is still one of Alan Silvestri's best works. I love the *End Titles* music with its saxophone part and the dynamic music for the action scene when Michael Douglas and Kathleen Turner are escaping in the jeep, the Little Mule.

New Yorker Alan Silvestri is best known for his music for *Back to The Future* and his collaboration with director Robert Zemeckis. *Back To The Future* (1985) is not Silvestri's best score, even though it is his most popular one. Among his collaborations with Zemeckis, Silvestri wrote the music for Arnold Schwarzenegger's *Predator* (1987), an amazing action-packed score, the sequel to Stephen Sommer's *The Mummy* (1999) called *The Mummy Returns* (2001), the first *Delta Force* (1986), *The Abyss* (1989), *Eraser* (1996), *Stuart Little* (1999), *Lara Croft* (2003), *Van Helsing* (2004), *Night of the Museum* (2006) and *The Avengers* (2012), to mention just a few.

For Robert Zemeckis's *Who Framed Robert Rabbit* (1988), a very ambitious live-action animated movie, Silvestri wrote perhaps his most sophisticated score. One of my favourite scores is also his music for the comedy *Mouse Hunt* (1997) which I wanted to discuss in my book as well, but did not have sufficient space for. For this film, therefore, take a look at my blog. *Mouse Trap* is a far better score than *Romancing The Stone*, but because this score is more popular and the first Silvestri score I ever heard, I decided to introduce the composer in my book with this one.

## The movie

*Romancing the Stone* was Robert Zemeckis's third movie and it started the frequent collaboration between the director and the composer Silvestri. The production history of this movie is very interesting. I read that 20th Century Fox expected the movie to be a flop after viewing a rough cut of it. Therefore, the producers fired Zemeckis as director of *Cocoon*, but *Romancing The Stone* became a surprise hit, earned over $86 million, launched Kathleen Turner to stardom and finally made Michael Douglas a star on the big screen. Danny DeVito had some great scenes in the movie and established himself as one of the leading comedians in Hollywood.

The success of this movie allowed Zemeckis to create *Back to the Future*, a movie that would be even more successful. I heard that Kathleen Turner and Zemeckis had a hard time working together, but the cast returned for a sequel that is unfortunately not as entertaining as the original one.

A comparison between this movie and Steven Spielberg's *Raiders of the Lost Ark* is obvious, but I think it is not fair to compare these two movies. Even though *Raiders* is a far better movie and *Romancing the Stone* sometimes has the quality of a B-movie, this film is still highly enjoyable and has some great funny scenes. When I was sitting with some friends in a pub in London, we were going through the movies of our childhood and we all loved *Romancing The Stone* and got scared by the scene when the bad guy lost his hand.

I also want to mention the story of the screenwriter. Diane Thomas was a waitress in Malibu who wrote the screenplay five years before production started. She died in a car crash shortly after the film's release, so it was her only screenplay. The novel based on the book was published under her name, but written by Catherine Lanigan. I have also read the book but it is not very good. I remember the awful written sex scene in the first pages, entirely off topic, and it nearly made me throw the book into the corner of my room. The last interesting fact to mention is that Sylvester Stallone was originally considered for the leading male role.

## The music

I have read[20] that in order to compete with the Steven Spielberg *Indiana Jones* movie, the score had to be more contemporary and reduce the orchestral action to a minimum. Silvestri impressed Zemeckis with his easy-going, jazzy and light rock ideas. Thus the music is clearly a product of the 1980s, but that is not a bad sign except for the use of synthetic percussion that I still do not like very much. Some critics on film music sites do not like the score because of its composing style, and I also have to admit that the score has just a few highlights, but these are highly enjoyable.

Varese produced a Club CD with 21 tracks. Let's go through this. The *Main Title* provides the theme and a nice sax arrangement. The next track *Elaine* underscores the kidnapping of Joan's sister, one of the typical 80s tracks on the score which I normally skip. I also skip the next two tracks *Ransacked Apartment I'm In Trouble,* I just like the percussion in this track.

With *Joan & Jack*, we hear the love theme in a nice but shorter arrangement. *The Gorge* is the first longer action track for one of the best scenes of the music. You can hear the typical way in which Silvestri builds up suspense, with drums and the brass section, and a sudden eruption of the full orchestra. This track shows perhaps the greatest difference between Silvestri and Williams in their writing of action pieces.

The best action track is the next track *Escape in the Little Mule*, for a highly entertaining action scene combined with some sightseeing in a very special way and a wicked sense of humour. The only problem with this track is that is too short, but this is because of the length of the scene in the movie which is also not very long.

*The Town* is source music for the carnival scene and I skip this track. *The Dance and They Kiss* is a funky arrangement of the main scene before it gets romantic. *Hotel Escape* is another action track, but not as entertaining as the *Mule* track, so I skip this too. *The Stone Revealed* is another track that I normally skip. *Mounties*, another action track, is similar to the *Mule* track, but nothing new yet I still really like it. *The Square* is source music again, so skip it, as is *Tregula*.

We have now the big action piece for the showdown. As a teenager, I was shocked by this violent scene with the crocodile that is unnecessary in my opinion. The music is interesting in its composing style, so I highly recommend listening to it.

*So Long Jack* is a romantic track and *The Sailboat* underscores the last scene of the movie with a funny joke. My favourite track of the score is the above-mentioned *End Titles* which combines the best parts of the score, and is highly enjoyable because of the saxophone and funky piano arrangements. This is a dancing piece and you can have great fun when you suddenly start playing it at a party. Some people remember the movie and a lively discussion ensues, but the younger generation who did not see the movie also mostly immediately switches into a dance mood...My plan is still to play this piece at my wedding...

You have to decide if you want to buy the score for just four or five really good tracks, but in my opinion the soundtrack is worth it.

# 10. Conan The Barbarian – An epic master piece

One intention of my book is also to talk about composers who might these days be forgotten. When thinking of film music, most people think of the big names such as Jerry Goldsmith, John Williams, James Horner, Bill Conti, Hans Zimmer and John Barry. If they are more sophisticated, they might perhaps also have heard of Elmer Bernstein, Rachel Portman and even Basil Poledouris. So, let's talk about him.

Basil Poledouris (1949 - 2006) was a Greek-American composer who won the Emmy for Best Musical Score for the TV miniseries *Lonesome Dove* (1989). Born in Kansas City, he was influenced by composer Miklós Rózsa, by his Greek Orthodox heritage and by the Russian classical composer Sergei Prokofiev. At USC, Poledouris met John Milius, the later director of *Conan The Barbarian*. Like Jerry Goldsmith, Poledouris worked with Paul Verhoeven on three movies: *Flesh and Blood* (1985, a wild historical action movie with Rutger Hauer and Jennifer Jason Leigh and now a cult movie), the original *RoboCop* (1987) and *Starship Troopers* (1997, the highly controversial and satirical bug-killing movie). Another very popular score by Poledouris is *The Hunt for Red October* (1990, perhaps the best Tom Clancy adaptation, with Sean Connery and Alec Baldwin), for which Poledouris composed a hymn that is similar to the Soviet Union's National Anthem.

Without doubt *Conan The Barbarian* is Poledouris's best score, but also check out his music for *Free Willy* (1993, the family drama about the friendship between a boy and an orca), *The Jungle Book* (1994, another live adaptation, this time directed by Stephen Sommers), *Les Misérables* (1998, Billy August's adaptation of the famous novel, this time with Liam Neeson and Uma Thurman) and the lovely score for *For Love of the Game* (1999, a baseball drama, directed by Sam Raimi with Kevin Costner).

## The movie

*Conan The Barbarian* was the movie that made Arnold Schwarzenegger a star. The Austrian's amazing career from bodybuilding to a movie star and then to the Governor of California is one of the most amazing life stories. When I was a teenager I preferred Stallone to Schwarzenegger, but with *Total*

*Recall* I started to become a big fan of Arnold Schwarzenegger. Finally, you have to admit that overall Arnie's movies are better, but because of *Rocky* and *Rambo* Stallone is a part of American culture, and out of my favourite movies there are more featuring Stallone than Schwarzenegger. I am particularly a big fan of the first two *The Expendables* movies.

In his autobiography, Schwarzenegger explained the making of *Conan* in a very entertaining way. This kind of movie would not be possible today because it is very rude, very violent and directed by a highly political director. John Milius, also the uncredited writer of *Dirty Harry* and the director of the great movie *The Wind and the Lion* (1975, for which Jerry Goldsmith wrote one of his finest scores), said in an interview: "I've always been considered a nut. They kind of tolerate me. It's certainly affected me. I've been blacklisted for a large part of my career because of my politics—as surely as any writer was blacklisted back in the 1950s. It's just that my politics are from the other side, and Hollywood always veers left." [21]

*Conan The Barbarian*, based on the stories of the pulp fiction writer Robert E. Howard from the 30s, is a fantasy action movie about a young barbarian who seeks revenge for the death of his parents. James Earl Jones, the voice of "Darth Vader", plays the bad guy called Thulsa Doom. Buzz Feitshans (who, for example, produced *Rambo I* to *III* and *Total Recall*) and Raffaella De Laurentiis produced the film for Dino De Laurentiis. The movie was very successful and earned more than $ 100 million. Of course, critics were not pleased and complained that the movie was advancing the themes of fascism. Totally off topic in my opinion because *Conan* is, very simply, the story of an individual fighting against a very bad guy who killed a lot of innocent people, therefore a typical Schwarzenegger or Stallone topic. Fascism? Oh, come on!

Schwarzenegger trained a lot to be prepared for the role. He took an 18-month training course before shooting began, and aside from running and lifting weights, he practised rope climbing, horseback riding, swimming and sword fighting. James Earl Jones helped Schwarzenegger a lot with deliver his lines in the right tone, as Schwarzenegger pointed out in his book. The producers made a huge effort to bring this fantasy world alive, with real decorations, miniature models and some effects by George Lucas Industrial Light & Magic. Even if you can sometimes see the effects, the movie is still fun to watch and highly enjoyable overall.

## The music

The score is one of the most crucial parts of the movie. Milius planed the film like an opera and therefore the music has a lot of choir tracks in it. Basil Poledouris, a friend of Milius, had successfully collaborated with the director before. Poledouris composed the music based on the storyboards and modified it through the recording. He also used a Musync, a music and tempo editing hardware and software system invented by Robert Randles, to modify the tempo of the compositions and finally synchronize them with the action in the film.

The starting point for the music was the melodic line that became well known as *Riddle Of Steel*. This music used massive brass, strings and percussion and became the Conan theme. Milius initially wanted a chorus based on Carl Orff's *Carmina Burana*, but after John Boorman's fantasy drama *Excalibur* (1981) had used Orff's work, Milius asked for an original score. The lyrics were composed in English and roughly translated into Latin, and the music was orchestrated by Greig McRitchie, Poledouris's frequent collaborator and an orchestrator who worked a lot for James Horner.

The theme of *Conan* is very popular, and Jerry Goldsmith used this theme later for *Total Recall*. I still have the Milan *Conan* CD of the soundtrack that consists of 12 tracks. Intrada released a three-CD box with the music, and a lot of more tracks can be found on that release.

Let's talk about a few tracks: *Prologue/Anvil of Crom* introduces the majestic theme for the movie, and it is interesting to compare this track with Goldsmith's main title for *Total Recall*. Track 2 *Riddle Of Steel/Riders Of Doom* is the first highlight of the score. After introducing a lovely melody, Poledouris underscores the attack of James Earl Jones and his warriors with a great action track and fabulous use of the choir. This is really amazing movie music!

There are a lot of great action tracks in this score such as the above-mentioned *Riddle Of Steel* and all the battle music (e.g. *The Kitchen/The Orgy, Battle of the Mounds*), but more lyrical tracks can be found such as *Atlantean Sword, Recovery* and the beautiful *Theology/Civilization*. Tracks such as *Wheel Of Pain* and *Gladiator* shows Poledouris's approach as underscoring this epic movie by using a lot of brass and more primitive rhythm to create music that is similar to the time of the plot. These tracks are not always easy listening music, but serve a great function in the movie. A lot of typical folk music can also be found in tracks such as *Escape from the Tower of Set*. In the end, you have to decide what you want: the original score in sound quality that is not up to date or the new recording by Nic Raine.

*Conan The Barbarian* is a clear product of its time as it reflects the political climate of the US in the 1980s with Ronald Reagan as president. Reagan emphasised the moral worth of the individual in his speeches, encouraging his fellow Americans to make the country successful and to stand up against the Soviet Union during the Cold War. Schwarzenegger was the perfect guy to convey this message as was Sylvester Stallone with *Rambo II* and *Rocky IV* (1985) when Rocky defeats the Russian boxer Drago, played by Dolph Lundgren, and in the end tries to convince the Soviet Politburo to change by giving a victory speech: "If I can change, and you can change, then everybody can change!"

Basil Poledouris's music for *Conan The Barbarian* ranks as one of the best film music scores ever and deservedly so. I like the second track most and have some trouble getting into the whole score, but the music is worth discovering again.

# 11. DRIVING MISS DAISY – THE HANS ZIMMER SOUND

When I started thinking about the contents for this book, I was sure that Hans Zimmer would be a big part of it. Hans Zimmer is a phenomenon. The German-born composer was able to create a new sound in the movie music business and dominates with his Remote Control Productions and the bunch of co-composers who are working with him on today's film music scene. With his very special combination of orchestra and synthesisers, Zimmer has created the Zimmer sound, and it is a sound that seems suitable for any movie genre.

Even though the success of Zimmer's music is very important for the business, it also has the side-effect that Zimmer is so popular these days that his name is now linked to nearly every recent blockbuster. I have a bunch of Hans Zimmer CDs in my collection, a lot of them I really love, but I also discovered that I have got a little bit tired of the typical overblown Hans Zimmer sound in the last few years and now choose the earlier and more lyrical ones. Zimmer composed some tracks that I highly admire, and in my opinion, his *Chevaliers De Sangreal* from *The Da Vinci Code* (2006) is one of the best film music tracks he has ever composed. When writing this book, I skipped more and more Hans Zimmer scores to discuss and finally just put two of them in my book, each for very special reasons.

To introduce Hans Zimmer here, I decided not to talk about *Gladiator* (2000, a score except the vocal parts I do not like very much) or some of his other overblown scores. When I was attending Hans Zimmer concerts in Mannheim, Germany in 2016 or at Wembley, London in 2017, I discovered that I like his lyrical ones more. I have a very special relationship with Hans Zimmer's score for *Driving Miss Daisy*. If I remember rightly, this was the first Hans Zimmer soundtrack I bought and it is still one of my favourites.

**The movie**

*Driving Miss Daisy* (1989) is an American comedy-drama adapted from the Alfred Uhry play of the same name. The film is directed by Bruce Beresford, with Morgan Freeman reprising his role as Hoke Colburn (whom he also portrayed in the play) and Jessica Tandy playing Miss Daisy. The story defines Miss Daisy's life, character and opinions by showing us her home and synagogue life, her conversations with friends and family, and her fears and concerns over a 25-year period. At the 62$^{nd}$ Academy Awards, *Driving Miss Daisy* received nine nominations, including Best Actor (Morgan Freeman), and won four awards: Best Picture, Best Actress (Jessica Tandy), Best Makeup and Best Adapted Screenplay.

The storytelling is convincing and the movie is a pleasure to watch. The characters are still light-hearted in their interactions, even though the author is revealing the prejudices against blacks and Jews in Georgia before the civil rights movement. Morgan Freeman is excellent in this role, and Jessica Tandy plays the old lady marvellously.

Hans Zimmer's main theme for the driving scenes gave the picture quite the right feel-good feeling and perfectly supports the emotions. I also used the score for my next long drive in a car a few days later and played the track *Driving* the whole time. It was a pretty nice drive!

**The music**

In my opinion, Hans Zimmer is much better at composing this kind of music than his bombastic action scores such as *Gladiator, Inception* or *Dark Knight.* *Driving Miss Daisy* seems to still have a special place in the composer's heart because he used the main theme as the opening cue for his concerts on the European concert tour Zimmer and his band are doing right now.

I attended the concert in Mannheim and it was quite fun to see the orchestra slowly coming on stage during this music. First, the theme started with the woodwinds, and the audience immediately recognised the score and praised the composer when he came on stage, sat at the synthesiser and played the famous theme.

Some critics were not happy about the fact that this score is electronic, without any "real" instrument in it, and that it does not focus much on the musical era at that time, except a slightly jazzy tone when Zimmer uses the sax and the clarinet. Personally, I do not understand the idea that for a movie set for example in the 1940s, you should only compose music from that time or in the musical style of that era. The movie is shot with modern equipment, so why not use modern instruments if the theme fits the tone of the movie?

Zimmer's heart-warming melody gives the movie exactly the right balance and the humour this story sometimes needed. Of all four tracks, the second one called *Home* is the weakest. It starts with some suspense, then switches to the lyrical part, this time with strings, and closes with the main theme again, with more piano on this track than on the others.

In the eight-minute-track *Georgia*, which underscores Mrs Daisy and Hoke's long drive, the best performance of the main theme can be heard with the use of more instruments, even though they were all sampled, and after one minute, there is a great jazzy arrangement with the sax before the synthesisers take over again. What a great moment in the score! Later in the track, there are some dissonant parts when Miss Daisy is alone in the car for a few minutes and gets worried. These dissonant tones can also be heard in Zimmer's score to *Pacific Heights* (1990). I usually skip this part.

The instrumental parts of the score with Hans Zimmer's music are just four tracks, roughly 25 minutes long, and in the last track called *End Title* there is a lovely reprise of the main theme, again with some lovely jazzy arrangements. For this score, Zimmer composed nice end credits music that summarises the most significant moments of the score.

*Driving Miss Daisy* is one of Hans Zimmer's best scores. It is very well composed, has a great and individual main theme and a score that works even without seeing the movie. This little lyrical score is much better than his action-packed scores from recent years and, in my opinion, Zimmer should go back to these more lyrical and quieter moments of his musical life.

## 12. "The past is the key to the future..." – An interview with Michael J. Lewis

One of the good aspects about writing a film music blog is that you sometimes develop very spontaneous ideas and try them out. I have always been a fan of Michael J. Lewis and remembered that he gave an interview to a German film music magazine that I very much enjoyed reading. I wanted to talk about Michael J. Lewis on my blog and decided to email him to see whether he would be interested in answering some questions I had. He was kind enough to do so, and therefore I include my interview with the composer which reveals his thoughtfulness and charming attitude here.

On his website (http://michaeljlewismusic.com) there is more information about the composer. Michael J. Lewis, born in 1939 in Wales, started his career as a choirboy aged six, became church organist at ten and later trained at the Guildhall School of Music and Drama in London where he studied harmony, counterpoint and composition. He scored his first movie *The Madwoman of Chaillot* (1968, starring Katherine Hepburn), a beautiful score for which he won the Ivor Novello Award for Best Film Score. Among his best known scores are *Julius Caesar* (1970), starring Charlton Heston, *The Medusa Touch* (1978), a great mystery thriller with Richard Burton, Lee Remick and Lino Ventura, *Theatre of Blood* (1973) with Vincent Price in one of his best roles, the thriller *North Sea Hijack* (1979) with Roger Moore and Anthony Perkins, the drama *The Man who Haunted Himself* (1970), an unconvincing thriller-drama with Roger Moore, and the Sydney Sheldon adaptation *The Naked Face* (1984), again with Roger Moore. One of Michael J. Lewis's best scores is the music to *The Lion, the Witch & the Wardrobe* (1979), an animation movie of C. S. Lewis's *The Chronicles of Narnia: The Lion, the Witch and the Wardrobe*.

*SR: Dear Mr Lewis, thank you so much for your kind words in your reply to my email and your willingness to answer a fan's questions.*

MJL: Thank you Stefan, for your intelligent and stimulating questions. It is my pleasure to provide answers to the best of my ability.

*SR: You said the greatest gift that a composer can have is the gift of melody. Is there a special way in which you approach a melody? I discovered that most of your themes are very lyrical and have a sense of solitude.*

MJL: The only approach I know to composition is making a daily attempt to overcome the fear that I may not write today as well as I did yesterday. The desire to better myself keeps my feet very firmly on the ground. One of the greatest melodists of all time, Wolfgang Amadeus Mozart, said: 'Melody is the essence of music'. I compare a good melodist to a fine racer, and counterpointists to hack post-horses; therefore, be advised, let well alone and remember the old Italian proverb: Chi sa più, meno sa – Who knows most, knows least. Many people have commented on the 'solitude' of my melodies. Some observers refer to the 'longing' feeling of my tunes. Others refer to the 'elegance' of my melodic lines. I have no problem with any of these comments. All I care is that people hear my tunes, whistle them, hum them, remember them and enrich their lives with them. For me, the art of composition is without doubt a solitary occupation. I do not want anyone near me when I write. It is essential that I am alone. No distractions. If that is reflected in my melodies, then that is the truth manifesting itself.

*SR: Two of my favourite scores are* The Island of Adventure *(1982) and* The Lion, The Witch, and The Wardrobe. *Can you tell me a little bit more about these two movies and your approach for the musical score? The second one is an animated movie, and I heard that composing music for animations might be more difficult than for feature movies. What is your idea about this?*

MJL: *Island of Adventure* was an attempt by a producer friend of mine to establish a film franchise based on the very popular British novels *The Famous Five* [by the famous author Enid Blyton]. Unfortunately, to the best of my knowledge, the result was not very fruitful, unlike the Emmy-winning *The Lion, the Witch and the Wardrobe* which gained great popularity all around the world and still generates a considerable volume of appreciative fan mail that I enjoy. Now parents, who as children, grew up on the score for *TLTWTW* and thereby discovered orchestral music are introducing their own offspring to my work. Very rewarding to know that my music makes a considerable contribution to peoples' lives far and wide. For me, scoring an animated film is no different to scoring a live action movie. Both genres have stories to tell, emotions to explore and sync points to catch.

*SR: Is there any musical influence from perhaps a classical composer? I assume you are not a big fan of the modern and atonal style and prefer more the classical or romantic composers such as Beethoven, Schubert or Bruckner?*

MJL: Sorry to tell you Stefan, but your assumption is not entirely correct! First of all, what is modern music? Is Stravinsky or Bernstein or Britten or Menotti modern? If so, I am very much a modernist. If Webern or Berg or Schoenberg are your idea of modernists, then I am not such a fan. We all learn from each successive musical period. Baroque led to Classical, which in turn became Romantic, leading to Neo-Classical. The late Romantic European music tradition of Mahler and Wagner certainly was a major influence on the early Hollywood film composers such as Tiomkin, Korngold and Steiner. Their influence is still very much alive in contemporary film scoring, no matter how disguised and diluted it may be. Wagner would have been an awesome film composer, but I am not sure how much work he would have got. Like many other great, true talents, the 'Hollywood experience' would have not have had much appeal to the independent, Bavarian master. If modern music is The Stones – great. But, they are not film composers!

*SR: Because I am a big fan of* The Medusa Touch, *can you tell me something more about your musical approach for this movie? It is one of the few scores that do not have a melody as a theme. In the track* Vibrations, *did you use some electronic instruments to achieve this haunting effect? And perhaps you can also tell me more about composing the track* Destruction Of Cathedral.

MJL: I did have a great fun writing the score. I felt that my principle task in scoring *Medusa* was to give the film much needed energy, spirit, vigour. The driving bass line of low strings, timpani, bass drum and pipe organ pedals went a long way to achieving that. Six of the finest London French horns were an enormous help. Wagner and Berlioz used eight, but in the studio six work very well. However, some years ago I did a Lowenbrau commercial that allowed me eight Wagner tubas (plus over a hundred other fine orchestral players). I did use a synth in the *Medusa* score but I am not a fan of electronics.

*SR: Of course, I have to ask about* Theatre of Blood. *The main theme is very lyrical, and I was surprised that you compose such a great theme for this kind of horror black comedy. Again, I think it is a musical expression of solitude. How did you approach this score?*

MJL: I am so glad about 'I was surprised that you compose such a great theme for this kind of horror black comedy'. All composers and writers seek to surprise the audience. The obvious can be so boring. If you regard the melody of *T of B* as 'a musical expression of solitude,' I am very pleased, because Lionheart, as an actor, would certainly have known solitude and loneliness. All creators do. I heartily recommend Randall Larson's notes to the recent CD re-release of *T of B*. Randall knows more about my music than I do! Your readers may like to know that a book devoted entirely to *T of B* is being published in London in September. I participated in a Q and A for the postlude.

*SR: What is your opinion about the generation of film music composers that are working today? In my opinion, Hans Zimmer changed the way of composing music and now we have these heavy electronic scores that sound to me like musical wallpaper. You really cannot separate the scores anymore because they all sound so similar. I attended a concert of Hans Zimmer in Mannheim, Germany a few weeks ago; it was fun, but he is more a rock music guy and not a classical composer, but I also remember that you said you love his score for* The Lion King. *Patrick Doyle is one composer who is composing in a more classical way with melodies and themes and not relying on heavy electronics. So, we have both ways these days.*

MJL: I do not wish to comment on the work of others. However, I will express my opinion about the era of 'heavy electronic scores' and scores that are generated by direct use of electronics, i.e. composition by keyboard rather than composition by traditional pencil and paper. I have done many recordings of my works by direct input via keyboards. The results can be amazing, but they frighten me because I truly believe something very essential is lost by by-passing the magic of deliberate thought that is then communicated by manuscript rather than a spontaneous, mental, almost improvisational method that is recorded instantly via the keyboard. I have a suspicion that the end result can be very clever but lacking in emotional essentials. This question is also at the heart of the digital/analogue debate. Purists believe that good old-fashioned magnetic tape has much more depth than the brilliance of digital. We all need to remember – the past is the key to the future.

*SR: And finally, I remember that Jerry Goldsmith said that he always wanted to compose the music for a Robin Hood movie, but never had the chance to do it. Is there any movie that you would love to compose the music for but have not yet had the chance to do it?*

MJL: I have been very blessed in scoring a wide variety of movies. But I do have a short wish list for the future and at the head of that list is my desire to score a superbly well-made, highly inspirational, very human film with a director and producer who fully understand the role and power of melody in film. Thinking of *Gone with the Wind* without its great melody is inconceivable, or *Breakfast at Tiffany's* without *Moon River*, *Exodus* without its soaring melody or *Zhivago* without *Lara's Theme*. One could almost be forgiven for crying out 'Bring back music'. As I said earlier – the past is the key to the future.

*SR: I would like to know what are your plans for the next weeks or months? I read about* The Romantic Splendour of Wales, *but have not yet had the chance to buy the CD, but I assume you moved away from film music scoring and are now doing something like writing the music you want to listen to? In earlier interviews you have referred to composing for film as catering to your 'mistress'. I still think you need a 'mistress'.*

MJL: Thank you for your generous suggestion, Stefan. Very interesting indeed. However, a composer needs to choose carefully, avoiding associating with one too big to have any energy, too thin to have any substance or insufficient intelligence to excite. Sometimes one just has to be patient and wait for the perfect opportunity to emerge and thrill. Actually, I have never moved away from film scoring; it's just that I have not received the right offer, creatively or financially for some time. I am a composer. Film is just a part of my creative repertoire. Each and every day I compose, and recently write as well. I find both activities madly addictive and all consuming. My plans for the future have never really changed. Very simply: every day I sit at my Bechstein Grand and search for the perfect melody that will be remembered for a thousand years. Additionally, I have been working for some considerable time on an original animated film musical with story, music and lyrics by myself. The initial anthropomorphic concept has now grown into a novel as well as a film. When my brain gets weary I go into my woods to be enchanted, invigorated and restored by the beautiful songs of my feathered friends in deepest Mississippi as I labour to reclaim open, peaceful, lush parkland from wild, dense jungle and reflect that – the past is the key to the future.

*SR: Thank you so much for your time and please stay well and safe!*

MJL: Appreciated. I will try.

# 13. Young Sherlock Holmes – Introducing Bruce Broughton

This is the only review of a soundtrack composed by Bruce Broughton in my book, but it was also the first movie with a score by Bruce Broughton I saw. *Young Sherlock Holmes* (1985) is a fantastic score, and Bruce Broughton is such a talented composer who film music enthusiasts have seemed to forget about in the last years. Recently Broughton has not been so involved in big blockbusters. Give this man the chance to work on another blockbuster! In the meantime, film music fans should think of putting his scores back into the CD player again.

## The composer

Because Bruce Broughton is not so popular these days, let's start with some information. Born in 1945 in Los Angeles and raised in Hawaii, Broughton graduated with distinction in 1967 from his music studies at the University of Southern California. He started to compose music for series such as *Gunsmoke*, *Quincy* and *Dallas*.

In 1984, he composed his first soundtrack for a feature movie called *The Ice Pirates*. One year later, he was nominated for an Academy Award for the first time for this score for *Silverado* (1985), directed by Lawrence Kasdan with Kevin Costner, Kevin Kline and Scott Glen. This is a wonderful western score and worth buying.

During his career, Broughton has received over 20 Emmy nominations and has won a record 10 Emmy awards, most recently for HBO's *Warm Springs* (2005), but also for *Glory & Honor* (1998), *O Pioneers!* (1992) and *Dallas: Ewing Blues* (1983). Major motion picture credits include *Lost in Space* (1998), *Tombstone* (1993, another western with a marvellous End Credits track), *Baby's Day Out* (1994, a lovely main theme and funny Micky Mousing), *Harry and The Hendersons* (1987, one of my all-time favourites scores), *Honey, I Blew Up The Kid* (1992), *The Boy Who Could Fly* (1986) and the two *Homeward Bound* movies (1993 and 1996).

## The movie

Also in 1985, Broughton composed the astonishing music for Barry Levinson's *Young Sherlock Holmes* and earned a Grammy nomination. This fantastic Sherlock Holmes adventure is one of my best childhood memories. Chris Columbus, who later directed *Home Alone* and *Harry Potter*, wrote a haunting screenplay about young Sherlock Holmes, played by unknown young Scottish actor Nicholas Rowe, who met his late friend John Watson for the first time at boarding school.

As a teenager, I started reading Arthur Conan Doyle's Sherlock Holmes stories and loved them. Even these days, I sometimes go back to them, and it is astonishing how popular Sherlock Holmes still is in short stories, movies and television. On Wikipedia, there is a statement by Columbus about what inspired him to do this story: "The thing that was most important to me was why Holmes became so cold and calculating, and why he was alone for the rest of his life. As a youngster, he was ruled by emotion, he fell in love with the love of his life, and because of what happens in this film, he becomes the person he was later."

I will not say what happened in the movie, so someone who has not already seen the movie can still enjoy it and will be surprised. The idea that Holmes and Watson did not meet first as adults in a chemical laboratory at St. Bartholomew's Hospital, as Arthur Conan Doyle explained in the first Holmes novel *A Study in Scarlet* (1887), is a fabulous idea and gives us a good insight into the personality of these two characters and why Holmes later became so cold, as Columbus explained.

Nicholas Rowe returned to the role of Sherlock Holmes 30 years later, in the 2015 film *Mr. Holmes*, in which he played the part in a movie that the "real" Mr Holmes, now a 93-year-old (played by Ian McKellen), goes to see at a theatre. Watson was played by Alan Cox, son of the actor Brian Cox. Sophie Ward plays Holmes' love interest Elizabeth, and Anthony Higgins gives an excellent performance as Professor Rathe. The movie has a great twist in the end, so watch it until the credits are finally over.

The film is also well known for including the first entirely computer-generated photorealistic, animated character, a knight composed of elements of a stained-glass window. When I saw this movie for the first time, I was highly impressed by this effect, created by Lucasfilm's John Lasseter, now the Chief Creative Officer at Pixar Animation Studio.

## The music

In 2014, Douglass Fake published a two-CD album with the music, and finally one of my childhood dreams came true. In San Francisco, where I lived at that time, I was finally able to listen to this music, and we have Intrada for making this release possible. In the booklet, there is an excellent interview by Intrada founder Fake with the composer. Broughton explained that he got the script while working on the western *Silverado* and pointed out that producer Steven Spielberg, who he met at the dubbing stage, liked the score.

I will mention a few titles of the beautiful soundtrack. Because of the setting of the score, the music is mostly composed romantically and harmonically, but for the hallucinations Broughton thought that extreme techniques were necessary. He was influenced by modern composers such as the German Hans Hermann Henze (1926-2012) and the Pole Krzysztof Penderecki (born 1933). In the interview Broughton explained the various themes. One, the *Investigating Theme*, is played by the piccolo and used for Holmes, another is called *The Adventure Theme* and is composed in a march style, a third theme is a fencing motif, then we have the love theme and, of course, the famous *Rame Tep* theme with choir.

The first track *The First Victim* underscores the opening, which soon turns into a shocking nightmare. When I was watching this scene as a teenager, I was both scared and highly impressed by the special effects and the haunting atmosphere. Some fans of the score say you can feel the influence of John Williams in this soundtrack. Comparing the scary moments of this first track with Williams's music for the first Indiana Jones, there are some similarities for sure, but Broughton did not copy Williams's music, he created his own musical style. The third track finally brings us the excellent main theme with sweeping strings and woodwinds before we can hear the majestic parts, played by the brass section.

The next track underscores *Watson's Arrival* and the first evidence of Holmes's smart mind, a very nice scene. I like very much the next small piece called *The Bear Riddle* because here you can hear the beautiful main theme played by woodwinds in a lovely interpretation, a short but highly enjoyable track.

*Library Love* introduces the love theme before we discover with *Fencing with Rattle* one of the highlights of the score. Holmes gets his first lesson in dealing with his emotions and suffers his loss against his antagonist Rattle. As Rattle explains: "Never replace discipline with emotion".

*The Glass Soldier* underscores the above-mentioned photorealistic character who attacks a priest. This three-minute piece is an excellent example of building up suspense with a traditional orchestra without using any electronic effects.

*Solving the Crime*, a fantastic scene in the movie with Holmes facing a riddle challenge, is another highlight. I could remember when watching the film how the audience's emotions for this scene were carried by Broughton's dramaturgical structure.

*Holmes and Elizabeth* brings us again a wonderful interpretation of the love theme. Without mentioning the plot of the movie, it is difficult to talk about the following tracks. So let me suggest that you will find the action music in *Pastries and Crypts* and *Temple Fire*, and the famous choir theme in *Rame Tep* and *Waxing Elizabeth* highly enjoyable.

In the extras of the CD, you can listen to the choir and the orchestral part of both tracks in separated pieces. This choral piece is an amazing track. Broughton explained in the interview that it was the first time he had used a chorus and he hired 16 singers.

With *Duel and Final Farewell*, Broughton underscores the showdown and the reason for Holmes's changing personality. Broughton's aggressive action track is highly artistic in its use of percussions and the more dominant brass section this time, not always easy listening music. The dramaturgical structure of this track is perfect, a real musical highlight, and with the love theme at the end also a beautiful ending to the story.

When I was a teenager, there were not many soundtracks available. So I sat with my tape recorder in front of our TV set and recorded the music from the movie. So, I watched the whole end credit scene and saw the last scene with the final twist. Columbus's idea to introduce Holmes's future nemesis, Prof. Moriarty, the "Napoleon of crime", is a great joke for the Sherlock Holmes fan community. At over six minutes, this final track is not only one of the longest tracks, but also one of the best. I admire Broughton's sense of composing lovely themes and melodies, something I sometimes miss in today's film music.

Unfortunately, the movie was not a big success at the box office, but it was and still is enjoyable to watch. With the chance to finally listen to the soundtrack album, you will have even more fun watching the movie than I had when I watched it the first time.

## 14. THE OMEN – A BLACK MASS

The Oscar! Finally! It was 1976, and Jerry Goldsmith won the long-deserved Academy Award. On YouTube, there is a video clip showing Jerry Goldsmith's shy joy and his words about his love for his wife, an adorable clip because you can see what a great personality Jerry Goldsmith had! I am pretty sure he never thought that this would be the only Academy Award he would ever win.

### The movie

*The Omen* is a British-American supernatural horror film directed by Richard Donner, the director of the *Lethal Weapon*-the franchise (1987-1998) with Mel Gibson and Danny Glover, but also the director of *Superman* (1978). *The Omen* was written by David Seltzer, who later wrote a novel from his screenplay, but compared to the movie the novel is not so convincing because the visual aspects of the film are much stronger. The book preceded the movie two weeks before as a marketing gimmick.

The film stars Gregory Peck as Ambassador Thorn, Lee Remick as his wife, David Warner as the photographer who has the best death scene in the movie, Harvey Spencer Stephens as Damien, Billie Whitelaw as the satanic Mrs Beelock and Patrick Troughton as Father Brennan.

I saw *The Omen* at the age of 18, and it made a great impression on me and, of course, I had tough nights afterwards.... This is a hell of a good movie and, as usual, the remake of such a classic is not. So why is the original *The Omen* so great? It is the rare combination of a terrific original script, Donner's great directing, the outstanding and convincing cast, and especially Jerry Goldsmith's music that made *The Omen* a horror classic. There is also an interesting documentary about the curse of *The Omen*, in my opinion, just a marketing stunt, but it is worth watching and you can find it on YouTube too.

According to producer Harvey Bernhard, the idea of a movie about the Antichrist came from Bob Munger, a friend of Bernhard's. When Munger told him about the concept, Bernard contacted screenwriter David Seltzer. It took a year for Seltzer to write the script. Gregory Peck was interested in this role because *The Omen* was more of a psychological thriller than a horror movie. Compared to John Carpenter's *Halloween* (1978), this might be true, but *The Omen* still has one of the most shocking death scenes of all horror movies, and I am pretty sure you all know which scene I am referring to.

## The music

During post-production, Donner and Bernhard asked Alan Ladd Jr., president of Twentieth Century Fox at that time, for more money to hire Jerry Goldsmith as the composer[22]. Donner and Bernhard listened to a concert by Jerry Goldsmith in the Hollywood Bowl and were impressed. Ladd agreed to an increase of $ 25,000 to hire Goldsmith, and the rest is history.

Jerry Goldsmith said in an interview that he heard choral voices in his head when seeing the movie, and so he developed the idea of this Latin chorale. Because he had not had that much experience with choral writing at that time, he asked Lionel Newman for help, who also conducted the music later.

Even though *The Omen* uses Latin chorales like in Carl Orff's *Carmina Burana*, it is a mistake to consider Jerry Goldsmith's soundtrack as a similar work. *The Omen* is more like a black mass. The refrain "Sanguis bibimus, corpus edimus, tolle corpus Satani" (ungrammatical Latin for "We drink the blood, we eat the flesh, raise the body of Satan") is used with alternating "Ave Satani!" and "Ave Versus Christus" ("Hail, Satan" and "Hail, Antichrist!"). The correct Latin would be "Sanguinem", but I think they used the wrong word because it is easier to pronounce and works better in the lyrics. You're all impressed with my Latin skills, right? [23]

*The Omen* is a great example of amazing movie music not only because of the use of the famous *Ave Satani*-theme, it is also a masterpiece in creating suspense and atmosphere with the traditional orchestra. You can argue whether the best soundtrack for a horror movie is Bernard Herrmann's *Psycho* or *The Omen*, but even though I love *Psycho,* I think *The Omen* is the better one.

Except for these suspense and action tracks in the score – I especially love how Goldsmith uses the bass in *The Dogs Attack* – you have one of Goldsmith's finest love themes that captures the love between Gregory Peck and Lee Remick before their life starts being destroyed by satanic forces. On

YouTube I found a great track of a live performance of *The Omen*, conducted by the Spanish film music enthusiast Diego Navarro, who conducts regular film music concerts in Europe. I like watching Navarro; he has so much fun with it and even speaks the word while conducting. Check it out!

For the 40th anniversary of The Omen, Varese Sarabande produced the ultimate CD of this soundtrack and added six cues that, although relatively brief, have been long awaited by fans of the score. I also bought the CD just because of these new tracks and especially for the track Mother's Death. This is the music that underscores Lee Remick's death, one of the best scenes in the movie and a great example of Richard Donner's sense of creating suspense. I am a fan of the first few notes of the track in particular. Even though you cannot see that Mrs Baylock has entered Kathy's room, it is clear that something dangerous is going to happen. When the camera finally shows her with the little sadistic smile on the face and Goldsmith's Satani music erupts, you know that Lee Remick's character will not survive the scene. This track alone is worth buying this edition for!

Jerry Goldsmith's *The Omen* and also the soundtracks to the other two movies are great examples of timeless movie music. The music to the third one is different from the previous ones because the new theme and the music to the showdown is more like an opera. Such a shame that it is composed for a bad movie. For an essential film music collection, *The Omen* and the music to the third one called *The Omen III: The Final Conflict* (1981, Damien is played by Sam Neill) cannot be excluded!

# 15. The Witches of Eastwick – Danse Macabre

*The Witches of Eastwick* (1987) is one of my favourite scores by John Williams. Based on a novel by John Updike, *Mad Max* director George Miller brought a fantastic cast together. Jack Nicholson as Daryl Van Horne gives one of his best performances, and Cher, Michelle Pfeiffer and Susan Sarandon play the three dissatisfied women who get seduced by Daryl the devil. John Williams's score is wonderful, and the *Dance of the Witches* is one of my all-time favourite tracks.

## The movie

Critics mentioned the differences between the movie and the novel from 1984. While the film follows the basic structure of the novel, the movie is not as dark as the book. The setting is still Rhode Island, but the book is set in the late 1960s. The book's plot is ultimately very different from the movie: the women share Daryl in peace until he unexpectedly marries their young, innocent friend Jenny. Through their magic the women ensure she gets cancer as revenge. The witches then doubt their judgment after Jenny's death when Daryl flees town with her younger brother, Chris, as his lover. The women are left in doubt about their actions. With the help of magic, each of them finds her ideal man and then leaves Eastwick. After seeing the movie, the book's plot, in particular the cancer idea, sounds horrible.

John Updike himself said the film "became Nicholson's movie and dissolved into special effects". And he further pointed out: "Perhaps my female characters have been too domestic, too adorable, too much what men wished them to be." For a writer who had been accused of not getting women then, this was a novel, he said, "about female power, a power that patriarchal societies have denied."[24] "Therefore, the book was considered as strongly pro-feminist and a rare case of a male novelist writing from women's points of view."[25] It is interesting is to note that Winston Graham's novel *Marnie* (1961) is also written by a woman's point of view, and Alfred Hitchcock directed his second and last Tippi Hedren movie based on this book.

By comparing the summary with the movie plot, it is clear that the movie plot is more fun, even though I think that some scenes just do not work, e.g. the tennis match is a little childish, and here Updike might be right that the movie dissolved into special effects. In the scene in the church when the witches start to take revenge on Daryl, the special effects work quite well and it is one of the funniest scenes in the movie, especially when Daryl complains: "Do you think God knew what he was doing when he created women?" With such a cast, you will not be disappointed watching the movie.

## The music

John Williams was again nominated for an Academy Award for this score, but this time did not win it. The soundtrack album consists of 14 tracks, and again I want to mention only a few. *The Witches of Eastwick* is Williams at his best and his sense of composing music for drama, comedy and darker moments fits perfectly well with this movie.

The basic motif is the *Dances of the Witches* (the second track and end titles), a modern version of the Dance Macabre. This Dance Macabre, or Dance of Death, is a genre of late medieval allegory on the universality of death. This Dance Macabre can be found in lyrics, pictures and classical music. They were produced as mementos mori to remind people of the fragility of their lives. No matter how happy you are, the Dance Macabre reminds you that Death is everywhere and you can die at any time. In the 19th century and with the romantic ideas in literature and music, the Dance Macabre became very popular, and composer such as Franz Liszt, Hector Berlioz and Camille Saint-Saëns composed famous musical arrangements. In movie music too, the Dance Macabre became very popular, e.g. Patrick Doyle used this theme in his score for *Needful Things* (1993) which I will discuss later.

John Williams's *Dances of the Witches* captures perfectly the dark humour and contrasts it with a slight comedy tone very obviously in the way in which Williams ends this piece: with a nice bow on the strings. The first track gives a nice introduction to the peaceful but also boring life in the city. Williams uses the strings and the piano to create a lovely atmosphere. Track 3 *Maleficio* is typical for Williams's more dramatic music. Track 4 *The Seduction of Alex* is the second masterpiece of this score. Williams builds up atmosphere and suspense while Daryl seduces Alex, and when she can no longer resist, the music erupts with an outburst of passionate music.

Track 6 *The Seduction of Suki and The Ballroom Scene* is the longest track and full of lovely melodies. Williams uses all the musical facets of an orchestra, and even though this track is nearly 30 years old, it still sounds fresh and lively. The next track is another highlight: *Daryl Arrives* underscores the turning point in the relationship between the three women and Daryl. The horns are used to give an idea that dark moments are coming soon.

Track 10 *Daryl rejected* is lovely in its use of the piano. Williams captures the feeling of Daryl's loneliness after none of the three women want to continue their relationship with him. Another action highlight comes right after with *The Ride Home*. The next two tracks bring the story to an end, and the last one is a reprise of the *Dance of the Witches*.

The movie is still very popular and ranks as one of the best fantasy comedies ever. George Miller is one hell of a director and proved with *Mad Max: Fury Road* (2015) that he can still create a blockbuster that attracts even the younger generation who perhaps have never heard of him before.

Williams is more popular because of his *Indiana Jones*, *Star Wars* and *Harry Potter* scores, but *The Witches of Eastwick* is a fabulous score, ranking with *Dracula* and *The Fury* as my top three scores by Williams.

# 16. MOONRAKER – JOHN BARRY'S BEST JAMES BOND SCORE

*Moonraker* is the first James Bond soundtrack reviewed in this book. None of the James Bond scores by John Barry has ever won an Academy Award! How could the academy ignore the fabulous soundtracks in this series? John Barry won five Oscars for his music, but never for James Bond. So let's talk about his best score in the franchise.

### The movie

*Moonraker* (1979) is the eleventh film in the James Bond series and the fourth to star Roger Moore. Lewis Gilbert was director for the third and last time, and it was Christopher Wood's second and last screenplay for a James Bond movie. With Lois Chiles as the Bond girl, James Bond finally has a smart and intelligent woman at his side[26], and Richard Kiel plays the killer Jaws for his second and final time. Michael Lonsdale as Drax gives a good performance, but he is not my favourite.

I read the novel a few years ago for the first time and was surprised by the large number of anti-German comments in the book. Hugo Drax is German of course, an ex-Nazi who wants to destroy London because Germany lost the war. A simply composed novel is always fun, right? All Germans are Nazis again and, how surprising, totally dumb. Some critics argue that the most convincing James Bond movies are the ones that are close to the books such as *Casino Royal* with Daniel Craig or *On Her Majesty's Secret Service*, and *Moonraker* was heavily criticised for developing a totally new story. But to be honest Ian Fleming's *Moonraker* is so boring that I had a hard time finishing it.

For the movie the plot was changed entirely, and because it was a French-coproduction the English actor James Mason was no longer considered for the role, and French actor Michael Lonsdale stepped it. Not a good choice, in my opinion, Mason would have been much better in this role. Remember how great he was in Alfred Hitchcock's *North by Northwest*?

Fleming had intended for *Moonraker* to become a film even before he completed the novel in 1954 since he based it on a screenplay manuscript he had written earlier. The film's producers had originally intended to film *For Your Eyes Only*, but the success of Steven Spielberg's *Close Encounters of the Third Kind* (1977) and George Lucas's *Star Wars* (same year) guided the way to *Moonraker* and an SF plot.

*Moonraker* received mixed reviews. Some fans think the movie is not serious enough (which is a problem of most Roger Moore Bond movies), the jokes are sometimes over the top (think of the Venice chase), and the space scenes in particular are not convincing. The quality of the movie seems to drop when Bond ends up going into space.

For me, *Moonraker* is my favourite Roger Moore Bond film, even though *The Spy who Loved Me* is a better action movie. *Moonraker* became the highest-grossing film of the series earning $210,300,000 worldwide, a record that stood until Pierce Brosnan's *GoldenEye* (1995).

If you look at the following James Bond movies in which Roger Moore played 007, only *For Your Eyes Only* (1981), which I will discuss later in my book, can be considered a good James Bond movie. *Octopussy* (1983) is boring at times and has just a few good scenes, and *A View To A Kill* (1985) is too violent, especially the massacre scene when Christopher Walken kills hundreds of people with a big smile and a laugh is not at all Bond-like.

## The music

*Moonraker* is the third and final collaboration between John Barry and Shirley Bassey. In my opinion, *Moonraker* is her best song because it is the most lyrical. *Goldfinger* is a classic and the most dynamic of the three, *Diamonds are forever* has some nice parts, but I like the timeless elegance of *Moonraker* more. Even though the lyrics sounds a little weird because Hal David had to put the word Moonraker into the song, I love it from the musical point of view. Kate Bush and Frank Sinatra were both considered for the vocals before Johnny Mathis was approached. Because Mathis was unable to complete the project, Bassey was hired, had just a few weeks before the premiere date in England and made the recordings at short notice.

In the introduction, I wrote that a lot of this book was about making choices. Discussing James Bond soundtracks is a perfect example of this, and each of us has a favourite score and reasons why it is precisely this score and not another one. In all, John Barry wrote the music to 11 James Bond movies and created the James Bond sound. *Goldfinger* (1964) is a classic and the benchmark for a good James Bond score, *From Russia with Love* (1963) and *On Her Majesty's Secret Service* (1969) are among my favourite James Bond soundtracks, and with his last Bond score, *The Living Daylights* (1987), Barry demonstrated that he was able to combine electronics and orchestra for action tracks in a modern James Bond setting, taking the James Bond music to a new level.

So why talk here about *Moonraker*? Because I think it is timelessly elegant in Barry's symphonic approach, especially when Bond is going into space. With this score, Barry made a switch in his composing style away from the jazzy style in his earlier scores with heavy brass to a slower musical approach here with considerable focus on the strings section. This more epic way of scoring was also used by the composer in *Out of Africa* (1985), which won John Barry another Academy Award for Best Score. This epic sound became John Barry's new trademark and earned him later another Academy Award a few years for the music in Kevin Costner's *Dances with Wolves* (1990).

*Moonraker* is very special in another way. There is not much use of the typical James Bond theme during the score. Instead, the composer used a piece called 007, the secondary Bond theme, which John Barry first introduced in *From Russia with Love*. A lot of classical music is used, too, for example, Drax plays Frédéric Chopin's Prelude no. 15 in D-flat major on the piano and Johann Strauss's Tritsch-Tratsch-Polka is used during the hovercraft scene on the Piazza San Marco in Venice. Film music fans will easily recognise Elmer Bernstein's theme from *The Magnificent Seven* (also in my book). And for insiders one last thing: the theme from *Close Encounters* was used as the key code for a security door.

The second track called *Space Laser Battle* is one of the highlights. I especially like the use of the choir here. Barry had never used a choir before in a James Bond score and would never do so again, but for *Moonraker* it was exactly the right approach. The choir gives the space scene a specific majestic atmosphere. Whether you like the scenes or not, this track is one of the best Barry ever composed for a James Bond soundtrack. Elegant, timeless and with great majestic strings.

Then you can hear the beautiful love theme in *Miss Goodhead Meets Bond* before we go into action with *Cable Car and Snake Fight*. At a running time of over six minutes, *Flight into Space* is the longest piece of the score, similar to *Space Laser Battle* in his elegant approach of using the strings. *Bond Arrives in Rio and Boat Chase* is another action highlight using Barry's James Bond theme. The last piece is a faster version of the *Moonraker* song, considered the disco version.

Music has always been a big part of the James Bond series, and the James Bond soundtracks should be an essential part of every soundtrack collection. With *Moonraker* you have one of the best James Bond soundtracks ever. I like Bill Conti's contribution to the series with *For Your Eyes Only*. David Arnold's James Bond soundtracks are perhaps the scores that best follow the John Barry tradition and took James Bond into the new century. Arnold's action pieces in particular have introduced a fresh attitude to the series, modern compositions but in the familiar James Bond style. I am not such a big fan however of Thomas Newman's contribution to the series.

John Barry will always be considered the perfect James Bond composer, and *Moonraker* is his masterpiece.

## 17. THE MISS MARPLE MOVIES – A CHILDHOOD MEMORY

When you ask people who are not film music enthusiasts "Who is Ron Goodwin?", you normally get a reply such as "I have no idea", but if you tell them he is the composer of the music for the four Miss Marple films with Margaret Rutherford, they immediately remember the song and the famous theme.

Ron Goodwin's music to these movies is a big part of my childhood. We had to wait until 2012 to finally get a good CD with the famous music, and I was as happy as a little child when I held this CD in my hands. Let's start with some basic comments about the author of Miss Marple, the four movies with Margaret Rutherford and the music of Ron Goodwin.

### Author Agatha Christie

Agatha Christie (1890-1976) is famous for her 66 detective novels and especially for creating the two very popular detectives Hercule Poirot and Miss Jane Marple. Agatha Christie also wrote *The Mousetrap,* the world's longest-running play, a murder mystery that is still on in London and that I watched years ago. Great fun! At the end of the play, the actors ask the audience to keep the secret of the murder so that other people can enjoy the play.

The Guinness Book of World Records lists Christie as the best-selling novelist of all time. Her novels have sold roughly two billion copies, and her works come third in the rankings of the world's most-widely published books, behind Shakespeare's works and the Bible. Christie remains the most-translated individual author, having been translated into at least 103 languages, and her crime novel *Then There Were None* is Christie's best-selling novel, with 100 million sales to date, making it the world's best-selling mystery ever. More than thirty feature films have been based on her work.

For all fans of Agatha Christie movies, there is another very popular theme, again by Ron Goodwin, this time for *The Alphabet Murders* (1965). The movie starring Tony Randall as Poirot is more a parody than a real crime movie. Goodwin's main theme is the best part of it and it can easily be found on YouTube.

## The Miss Marple movies with Margaret Rutherford

Although Miss Marple has been portrayed by other actresses (e.g. Angela Lansbury and Helen Hayes), Margaret Rutherford's performance is the most popular one.

The character of Jane Marple had previously featured in short stories, but *The Murder at the Vicarage* (1930) is the first real Miss Marple novel. Never married and with no close living relatives except a nephew, Miss Marple can be considered a female version of the typical single British detective fiction, the so-called gentleman detective, in contrast to the hard-boiled detectives in Dashiell Hammett's novel such as *The Maltese Falcon* (1930) or Raymond Chandler's Philip Marlow.

Popular from her first appearance, Jane Marple had to wait thirty-two years for her first big-screen appearance starring Margaret Rutherford, who changed the characteristics of the popular detective. The four movies with Margaret Rutherford were very popular light comedies, but were disappointing to Agatha Christie because Rutherford's performance was very different from the Miss Marple in the books. As a tribute to Rutherford's performance, Agatha Christie dedicated the novel *The Mirror Crack'd from Side to Side* (1962) to the actress, "in admiration". Margaret Rutherford played Miss Marple as an eccentric and self-reliant old lady and insisted that her husband, Stringer Davis, played a role in the movies, becoming Miss Marple's Dr Watson.

*Murder, She Said* (1961) was the first of four British MGM productions starring Margaret Rutherford, all directed by George Pollock. This first film was based on the novel *4:50 from Paddington* (U.S. title *What Mrs. McGillicuddy Saw!*, 1957), and the changes made to the plot, for example adding Mr Stringer and describing Miss Marple as more active, were typical for the series. In the film, Mrs McGillicuddy is cut from the plot and it is Miss Marple herself who sees the murder committed on the train alongside hers. Because she was reading a crime novel, the police did not believe her and thought she was day-dreaming.

The other three films of the series were *Murder at the Gallop* (1963), based on the Hercule Poirot novel *After the Funeral, Murder Most Foul* (1964), based on the Poirot novel *Mrs. McGinty's Dead*, and *Murder Ahoy!* (1964), not based on any Christie work, but incorporating a few plot elements from *They Do It With Mirrors* (1952).

## The music by Ron Goodwin

Ron Goodwin (1925-2003) was an English composer known for his music for over 70 films in a career lasting over fifty years. His most famous works included *Where Eagles Dare* (1968, one of the best Alistair MacLean's adaptations), *Battle of Britain* (1969), *Of Human Bondage* (1964), *Operation Crossbow* (1965) and *The Magnificent Men in their Flying Machines* (1965). He even worked with Alfred Hitchcock on *Frenzy* (1972) and replaced a score by Henri Mancini.

The Miss Marple theme became one of Ron Goodwin's most popular themes, and it took soundtrack companies until 1992 to release an album with the score. Goodwin used the famous theme for all four Miss Marple films, each time with slight variations. This main theme is composed in a Rococo style that has a distinct 1960s feeling and is known to be a highly complex piece of music due to the quick playing of the violin and the harpsichord. Goodwin was approached by director Pollock after he heard about him from Stanley Black, who had worked with Pollock on *Stranger in Town* (1957) and had used Goodwin as his orchestrator many years previously[27].

When I watched these four Miss Marple movies as a teenager, I connected my tape recorder again to the TV set and recorded the title theme, giving me one of my first experiences of movie music. For the suite on the CD, Goodwin had to recreate the music because the original sketches had been destroyed, like a lot of other sketches from that time.

The new recording is very nice and very close to the originals ven though the percussion is more dominant. Goodwin mostly used material from *Murder Ahoy!* and *Murder at The Gallop* (the hunting theme with the horn). Except for this Miss Marple suite, there are other suites on the CD but I normally skip them. These suites feature music for *Lancelot and Guinevere* (1963) and *Force Ten from Navarone* (1978), the sequel to the very popular *Guns from Navarone* (1961, both by Alistair MacLean). Maybe Goodwin thought that a full CD with just the Miss Marple music would be too boring, and perhaps he was right in not doing it.

Ron Goodwin's music for these four Miss Marple movies is an excellent example of timeless movie music. Even though the tone is mostly light, such as in comedy music, Goodwin was able to create haunting and suspenseful music for the series and underscored the few very dramatic scenes quite well. The main theme though has become one of the most popular themes in film music history.

# 18. The Burbs – Jerry Goldsmith's best score?

Jerry Goldsmith's soundtrack to *The 'Burbs* is one of the best scores he ever composed, and in my opinion one of the best soundtracks ever. This soundtrack is so full of ideas that it is a pleasure to listen to this score over and over again, especially the *End Credits* music, which is an astonishing track.

*The 'Burbs* is a small and underappreciated movie from a time when Tom Hanks was not the iconic star he is today. The cast is exceptional, the script full of weird humour, and Goldsmith's score is so enjoyable that you have to listen to it a number of times to discover and appreciate all the funny moments and musical jokes.

## The movie

Joe "Gremlins" Dante directed this comedy in 1989 with a lot of satirical but also horror elements, and continued the very successful collaboration with Jerry Goldsmith by working on this picture. Their collaboration was exceptionally successful, and for Dante Goldsmith composed his last soundtrack *Lonely Tunes Back in Action* before he died of cancer in 2004.

*The 'Burbs*, based on a screenplay by Dana Olsen, makes fun of living in a suburban environment. On Wikipedia, you can read a quote by the author: "I had an ultra-normal middle-class upbringing, but our town had its share of psychos. There was a legendary hatchet murder in the thirties. As a kid, it was fascinating to think that Mr XY down the street could turn out to be Jack the Ripper."

When I wrote a review of this score for my blog, I was living in San Francisco and could appreciate the humour of the movie even more. One of my friends living in one of these typical suburban areas told me that life there is as dull as it is portrayed in the film. He was telling me of a neighbour who threw old shoes at the house when my friend partied too loudly.

Tom Hanks played the lead male role, his wife is portrayed by Carrie Fisher, Bruce Dern gives a marvellous portrait of a war veteran. When new neighbours called Klopeck arrive in the city and start doing their strange stuff, Hanks and co. begin to investigate. Finally, some action in the boring neighbourhood!

As I remember, the Klopecks speak English with a German accent. Okay, blame the Germans again, always a good idea. Henry Gibson, one of the judges in the famous law series *Boston Legal*, is marvellously bizarre as the head of the Klopeck family. I won't say what happens in the plot and especially at the end, so you can all enjoy the movie if you have not seen it.

## The music

Jerry Goldsmith's music is a firework of ideas! The soundtrack is a great example of how he was able to combine a classical orchestra with modern electronics. If you want to buy just one soundtrack, then buy this one in the "Deluxe Edition" because it is a perfect example of what movie music can do when a gifted composer such as Jerry Goldsmith is working on a picture.

There are so many great tracks in this score that it is difficult to mention just a few. One of my favourites is called *My Neighbourhood*. In this two minute-piece, Goldsmith composed a parody of his famous *Patton* (1970) score – the trumpet-echo motif – and also used a special instrument to make some squeaky noise. This works wonderfully in the film scene. You can also find music similar to another famous Goldsmith score in *The 'Burbs*: in the second track called *The Window/Home Delivery* Goldsmith composed typical music for American suburban life, similar to the music in *Poltergeist*. You can also hear the musical barking of a dog. These quirky ideas make this score outstanding and highly enjoyable.

The first track *Night Work (Main Title)* sets the tone for the gothic moments of the score with the organ from 1'01. You know that something scary will happen! This track also introduces the *Patton* parody, used as a theme for Bruce Dern's character. The organ, the motif for the *Neighbours from Hell*, is used in various tracks and brings a gothic horror feeling to the score. The highlights are track 5 *Good Neighbours*, a scene composed as if in a Sergio Leone western, and *Let's Go*, a great parody of typical Ennio Morricone western music, even with gunshots. This track has a funny ending when the visit does not have the expected result and bees attack Hanks and his friends.

One of the longer tracks is track 10 *The Garage*, which perfectly captures the horror style of the movie. The scene is brilliantly shot with its totally over-the-top approach as you see what the Klopecks are doing with their rubbish on a rainy night. Neighbours from hell? After this scene, you start to believe it. Another highlight is the music for the dream sequence. The two tracks are *Devil Worship* and *The Dream*. Goldsmith builds up some suspense first with strings and drums, then a violin is played in a Paganini devil player style combined with a female voice in the style of a mythical figure, and then the organ is used again. This track is perfect musical underscoring for a bizarre scene that results in Tom Hanks's nervous breakdown.

When Hanks and his cohort start searching the Klopeck house, we are reaching another musical highlight with *The Wig*. Bruce Dern has some of his best moments so the *Patton* parody is heavily used. The following tracks use the material already introduced and are sometimes very dependent on the scenes. Another highlight among these tracks is *Something is moving* which combines all the musical themes.

Some critics did not like the ending of the movie with the final twist. Goldsmith starts to underscore these scenes with *My Skull/The Gurney* and some nice action music. *Pack your Bags*, the second last track, is a more lyrical one after the mystery is solved, and then we have with *Square One (End Credits)* the best track of the whole CD. With this four-minute piece, Goldsmith created a musical firework and the perfect end credits music for this score. He used all the various themes – the lovely suburban theme, the gothic horror theme, the western theme and the heroic war theme – and brings the album to a great ending.

The musical structure of this piece is highly complex with nearly three layers in the music. Listen in particular to the way the strings are played in the background before the organ starts to play. This track is one of my most favourite tracks ever, and when you listen to this music you can understand why Jerry Goldsmith is my favourite film music composer. He had so much to offer!

It seems that this soundtrack is pretty tricky to obtain, but do try and buy it, especially the "Deluxe Edition". It is worth every penny. It is a shame but not surprising that Goldsmith was not even nominated for an Academy Award with this soundtrack, but remember even Bernard Herrmann's *Psycho* was not nominated. *The 'Burbs* is astonishing movie music and my favourite Jerry

Goldsmith score.

## 19. Star Trek 2 – The Wrath of Khan – James Horner's masterpiece

I gave considerable thought to which score by James Horner should be the subject of a second review of his music. As mentioned in *Aliens*, I was introduced to James Horner by another soundtrack enthusiast, and he recommended that I buy *Willow*, a fantasy movie by Ron Howard starring Val Kilmer. This movie is long forgotten, but the music is still very popular among Horner fans. When listening to *Willow*, I was immediately impressed by Horner's lovely themes and the very dynamic action tracks.

So why not include *Willow* here? Because I decided to talk instead about James Horner's more famous scores, and two of them are *Aliens* and this score for *Star Trek 2 – The Wrath Of Khan* (1982), for me the second-best movie in the *Star Trek* franchise. I like *First Contact* (1996) most because of the haunting atmosphere and Jerry Goldsmith's astonishing score.

The reason for talking about *Star Trek 2* on my blog was the death of Leonard Nimoy in Los Angeles on 25 February 2015. The success of the second *Star Trek* movie and Horner's score lifted the composer immediately to Hollywood's A-list of composers. When Universal Studios redesigned their logo in 1990, Horner was asked to compose a fanfare, and these few seconds capture the magic of movies in a beautiful way.

### The movie

I always preferred the original *Star Trek* series to the other ones, especially to *The Next Generation*. Of course, Patrick Steward gave a great performance as Jean-Luc Picard, and the effects and even the storytelling were better. For example the episodes about Locutus are amazing. So, why do I still like the original one better? Mostly because of Spock, this fascinating character with his special mix of pure logic and emotions because of his human side. *The Next Generation* tried to create someone similar with Data, but there is just one Spock.

I also think that the humour in the original series is much better. Remember the Tribbles episode or the constant fighting between McCoy and Spock. Leonard Nimoy played his character so well that there were rumours that

Shatner was jealous because Spock became more popular than his Captain Kirk. On YouTube there are a great many fan tributes, with jokes and comments about the original one. Yesterday, I watched a hilarious one about the unique fighting style of Kirk, e.g. the double first. Check this funny video out!

In the second movie the producers wanted to go into a different direction. The first movie was successful, but critics considered the plot too thin for a whole film. There were also not many action scenes, and it was overwhelmed by philosophy. So Harve Bennett became the new producer, Gene Roddenberry had to step back, and Nicholas Meyer wrote the script and directed. His idea of creating a second story about the famous character Khan played by Ricardo Montalbán was a great idea.

There was not enough money to hire Jerry Goldsmith again. His score for the first *Star Trek* movie was highly praised and rates as one of his best and most popular works. I will also discuss this score later in my book. For the second movie, James Horner stepped in and, as in *Aliens*, he again composed the music for the second movie of a series whose initial composer was Jerry Goldsmith.

## The music

James Horner's score is considered one of his best works. Some fans also think it is the best soundtrack of the whole series. *Star Trek 2: The Wrath of Khan* is still a highly enjoyable movie, and Horner's music makes an excellent contribution to the franchise with its fresh musical ideas. Also, starting with this soundtrack, Horner began copying from his own earlier soundtracks. Nevertheless, the melodies and action music create an epic atmosphere. Horner demonstrated that he was one of the best composers of the upcoming generation of film music composers at that time.

Let's start with the *Main Title*. In an interview[28], Meyer said that he was tired of the march music in SF movies. His idea was that Horner, at that time 28 years old, should emphasise more the aspects of sea journeys and swashbuckling. Horner created a score that is reminiscent of Erich Wolfgang Korngold.

Horner created a new main theme and went straight to action with the second track called *Surprise Attack*. In this five-minute track, Horner produces a fantastic piece of music with some atonal effects, a lot of different percussions and beautiful melodies.

There is plenty of outstanding action music in this soundtrack, for example the fourth track *Kirk's Explosive Reply* and especially *Battle in the Mutara Nebula*, which is over eight minutes long. Not just on the screen and in combination with the movie, these pieces are highly enjoyable. Horner is best when he can demonstrate his ability to deal with the full force of a big orchestra. *Khan's Pets* brings us the motif for Khan, the music is haunting and dangerous to emphasise Khan's insanity. In contrast, the short piece called *Spock* focuses on the human side of Spock.

*Enterprise Clears Moorings* is another beautiful piece that starts with the new Star Trek melody. *Genesis Countdown* is again a longer track, over six minutes long, and has a dramaturgical structure that is just mind-blowing. Horner at his best! *Epilogue/End Title* (you can hear Nimoy's voice) is the longest piece, an epic track that brings the soundtrack to a great ending.

The score was written in four weeks, and an orchestra of 91 people played the music. The length of the total music in the movie is 72 minutes. The music was a huge success and is very popular among James Horner fans and fans of the *Star Trek* franchise.

James Horner composed the music for the next *Star Trek* movie, but it is not as good as the *Wrath of Khan* and some parts of the *Stealing the Enterprise* track are very similar to Sergei Prokofiev's ballet *Romeo and Juliet*. Therefore, *The Wrath of Khan* is James Horner's best contribution to the Star Trek franchise and perhaps his best contribution to the SF genre in general.

# 20. ROCKY – BORN OF A LEGEND

*Rocky* is part of American history. It is the movie that made Sylvester Stallone famous, it is the movie that made composer Bill Conti famous, and it is still one of the best sports movies ever. So it is time now to talk about the *Rocky* franchise.

One of the rules I set for my blog from the outset was that I would talk just about one score from a franchise when the composer was the same. Therefore, I will not review the other *Rocky* scores in a separate review, even though I think that the best tracks from the franchise feature in the score for *Rocky 2* and *Rocky 3*, and even *Rocky 5* has one track that is very nice during the fight scene at the end. For my book, I have followed this principle, but added additional information to this review and rewrote it overall.

## The movie

*Rocky* is a 1976 American sports drama film directed by John G. Avildsen and both written by and starring Sylvester Stallone. It tells the typical American Dream story: Rocky Balboa is an uneducated but kind-hearted working-class Italian-American boxer. He works as a debt collector for a loan shark in the slums of Philadelphia and gets the chance to fight against the heavyweight boxing champion, played by Carl Weathers who later joined Arnold Schwarzenegger in hunting the *Predator* (1987).

Most film fans know the story that Stallone was inspired by the fight between Muhammad Ali and Chuck Wepner, "The Bayonne Bleeder". Chuck was able to fight fifteen rounds against Ali and was not knocked out early as boxing experts had supposed. He even hit Ali very hard in the ninth round, a scene also found in the *Rocky* movie.

Producers liked the story but not seeing the unknown Stallone in the role. Stallone fought for his project and the rest is history. The film, made on a budget of just over $1 million and shot in 28 days, was a sleeper hit and eventually earned $225 million in global box office receipts, becoming the highest-grossing film of 1976. *Rocky* went on to win three Oscars, including Best Picture. The movie is considered one of the greatest sports films ever made and was ranked as the second best in the genre, after Martin Scorsese's

*Raging Bull* (1980, with Robert De Niro as Jake LaMotta), by the American Film Institute in 2008.

*Rocky* started a franchise with six sequels: *Rocky II* (1979), *Rocky III* (1982), *Rocky IV* (1985), *Rocky V* (1990), and *Rocky Balboa* (2006) as a final chapter, directed again by Stallone, with *Creed* (2015) as an unofficial sequel but continuing the story and bringing it to an end. Stallone portrays Rocky in all the sequels, wrote the scripts for all of them (except *Creed*) and directed four (Avildsen returned to direct *Rocky V*, and Ryan Coogler directed *Creed*).

Out of all the movies, I like *Rocky III* best because I think it has the best story about an arrogant fallen champion who underestimates his opponent, has lost his appetite (*Eye of the Tiger*), is afraid of losing again in a revenge fight, but fights his demons with the help of a friend and former opponent and finally wins. This is a great storyline and proves that Stallone is a great screenwriter. Bill Conti composed his best score for *Rocky III*, especially in the quieter parts of the movie such as the track *Mickey*. *Rocky II* offers Conti's best action track for the whole series with *Conquest*, while the track for the final part in *Rocky V* is a modern version of it with contemporary elements.

I grew up with the *Rocky* movies and cannot count how often I have seen them. The *Rocky* movies are not only an inspiring story, but are also great for your own motivation. Never give up, always stand up after a "punch in the face" and keep going until you succeed and finally reach your goals. What better phrase to motivate you can there be?

### The music

Bill Conti had worked with the director before and composed a score for *W.W. and the Dixie Dancekings* (1975) that was rejected by the studio, as Conti explained in an interview with *Emmy TV Legends*. In the interview Conti also explained that composer David Shire, at that time Talia Shire's husband, was not composing the music for *Rocky*. Conti did not know why, then another guy also could not do it, so Avildsen finally reached out to Conti again due to the film's relatively low budget. "The budget for the music was 25 grand," said Avildsen. "And that was for everything: the composer's fee, that was to pay the musicians, that was to rent the studio, that was to buy the tape that it was going to be recorded on." Conti therefore recorded the music in one three-hour session.

Each film music fan considers *Rocky* as one of the most amazing movie soundtracks ever. When Rocky is running up the steps to the Museum of Modern Art in Philadelphia, you are still impressed by the energy of this scene combined with the powerful score by Conti. The main theme song, *Gonna Fly Now*, was placed by the American Film Institute at 58th on its AFI's 100 Years...100 Songs.

*Rocky* is like John Williams's score for *Indiana Jones*: a simple, but powerfully composed score with a characteristic motif that can easily be played on the piano. The music is pure Italian – both Conti and Rocky have Italian origins – in its sense of combining a lovely melody with melodramatic aspects. *Rocky* is last but not least also a product of the 70s in the use of electric guitars. Even after 40 years, the training music has so such energy that you can easily use it for your training and weightlifting and have a perfect rhythm for your own pumping iron.

There is a great clip on YouTube with Bill Conti playing the famous *Gonna Fly Now* on the piano. Conti explained that this song was not actually planed as a song; it came about by adding different pieces together. John Avildsen came to Conti and said he needed nearly 90 seconds for the training music. So, Conti composed the fanfare and went over to the beat. Avildsen needed more music because he did not use the medicine ball and wanted to add some push-ups, so Conti composed more, then the director needed another 30 seconds and another 30 seconds. So, Conti began adding these pieces together and it became the now famous song.

A great example of composing a piece of unforgettable music!

## 21. HELLRAISER – A MODERN GOTHIC HORROR SCORE

I was introduced to Christopher Young by another film music enthusiast. As I will explain later, I am not a big fan of modern horror movies, and because Young was composing a lot of music for these movies he was not on my agenda. My friend suggested buying Young's *Hellraiser* (1987) even without seeing the film, and I was highly impressed by its score. Since then I have watched some crappy movies just because Young composed the music for it.

Young is a composer who film music enthusiasts should rediscover. I have a few soundtracks by him in my collection, and mostly have not watched the movies these scores were composed for. As *Hellraiser* is the score that made Christopher Young popular, I wanted to introduce this composer in my book with this soundtrack.

Other scores you should check out are *The Fly II* (1989, the first one was composed by Howard Shore), *Flowers in the Attic* (1987, a more lyrical one), *Hellbound – Hellraiser II* (1988), *Murder in the First* (1995, a fantastic score!), *Copycat* (1995, some very good action music in it for a rude but also very good serial killer movie with Sigourney Weaver) and *Spiderman 3* (2007, co-composed with Danny Elfman). Christopher Young has a website featuring tracks of this score at http://officialchristopheryoung.com/music. I asked him for an interview via email but did not receive a reply.

**The composer**

Christopher Young was born in Red Bank, New Jersey, in 1958 and he graduated from Hampshire College in Massachusetts with a Bachelor of Arts in music. He then completed his postgraduate work at North Texas State University and moved to Los Angeles in 1980.

Originally a jazz drummer, he decided to become a film composer when he heard Bernard Herrmann's music, and then studied at the UCLA Film School under the famous film composer David Raksin. Young now teaches at the Thornton School of Music of the University of Southern California[29].

Young's contribution to the horror genre is astonishing. I remember when I first heard the music for *Hellraiser* how impressed I was that at last here is an artist again who knows how to use an orchestra and does not just take a synthesiser to make some electronic noise and later call it film music.

Recently Young has scored a lot of the music for the third *Spiderman* by Sam Raimi. The background story is a little complicated, but it seems that Elfman and Raimi did not get along very well and Young was hired, but then Elfman stepped in again, so there is now the music of both composers in this movie. Unfortunately, there is no soundtrack album with Christopher Young's music available, even though his motif for the sand man (*Birth of a Sandman*) is a marvellous piece of music.

Young has composed very modern music for the horror movies he has worked on. It is not always easy listening, but he has such a great talent to underscore these violent movies with a special atmosphere that I watched two of them to have a better understanding of the music.

## The movie

*Hellraiser* (1987) is a British horror film, written and directed by Clive Barker, based on his book *The Hellbound Heart*. I am not generally a big fan of modern horror movies and prefer the old classics from the 40s to the 60s. Most modern horror movies are too violent for me. Often, I get the feeling that makeup artists such as Tom Savini (which worked on George A. Romero's *Dawn of the Dead*, 1978) are the real creative people behind, and the only intention of these movies is to see how long people can stand watching them without going to the restroom to vomit. Therefore *Hellraiser* was praised because it made a difference and really tells a story.

*Hellraiser* is also full of violent scenes and shocking effects, but it has a good story and with Pinhead created one of the fascinating figures of the modern horror genre. Furthermore, Barker has a great feeling for building up suspense and creating plot twists. He had some trouble with some violent scenes, but also with nudity, as he explained in an interview with the magazine Smahain: "Well, we did have a slight problem with the eroticism. I shot a much hotter flashback sequence than they would allow us to cut in.... Mine was more explicit and less violent. They wanted to substitute one kind of undertow for another. I had a much more explicit sexual encounter between Frank and Julia, with some spanking, but they said no, let's take out the sodomy and put in the flick knife." [30]

The main gadget of the *Hellraiser* series is a puzzle box. In the first *Hellraiser* movie, the main male character Frank Cotton buys the box in Morocco, and when he solves the puzzle, hooked chains emerge and tear into his flesh. The following story is another variation of the classical vampire motif, but it is the way Barker tells his story that makes *Hellraiser* a classic of modern horror movies. The movie cost $1 million and made $14 million. Quite impressive, isn't it?

## The music

Barker initially wanted the British electronic band Coil to compose the soundtrack, but this idea was rejected so editor Tony Randel suggested Christopher Young. Another interesting fact I found was that there was a big discussion about the title. Barker suggested *Sadomasochists from Beyond the Grave*, and one woman on the team really did suggest this title: *What a Woman Will Do for a Good Fuck* [31].

Young's music offers a great mix of lyrical themes and shocking atonal and avant-garde music. The main theme is an excellent example of a haunting theme that you will not ever forget once you have heard it. The second track called *Resurrection* is the first highlight of the score. Young creates a haunting atmosphere with strings, brass and percussion. This piece underscores one of the most important scenes in the movie and is highly enjoyable.

Track four, *The Lament Configuration*, is a good example of the modern electronic effects Young likes to use in his scores. Another example is *Seduction and Pursuit*, a piece that starts first with the motif for the Cenobites and then continues with music composed in a highly modern style. Not easy listening, but fascinating when you see how this music works in the movie. Similar to the music you can hear in *Cenobites*, Young transformed the noise of the chains into music and created some additional music for the creatures from beyond.

The last four tracks are the final highlights of the score. Young uses the motif he introduced in *Resurrection* for the track *Re-Resurrection*. Again, you have to imagine the time when this score was composed. Young brought an orchestra and lyrical themes back to the horror genre, which was mostly dominated by heavy metal or lousy synthesiser scores, and we really have to be grateful for Young's approach.

With *Uncle Frank* the showdown starts. Young uses the brass and string section to underscore the following violent scenes. *Another Puzzle* is the last track of the score, a very lyrical track, and because of the title you can imagine that the final scenes are not the end of the Cenobites and the *Hellraiser* story.

The next movie *Hellbound* was more violent and has a lack of good storytelling. The positive thing is that we learn more about Pinhead in the beginning and can see how he was created. Young's music is the best aspect of this movie. He used the themes from the first one, but also a choir and again highly modern and even more avant-garde music. Christopher Young's two *Hellraiser* scores are milestones in modern horror film music, so I highly recommend listening to them.

## 22. NEEDFUL THINGS – ART AND THE MINISTER

*Needful Things* is one of Stephen King's best novels. Even though King is not one of my favourite authors, I have read a few of his books, for example *It*, *Needful Things*, *Pet Sematary*, *The Stand*, *11/22/63* (King's best love story) and *Under the Dome* (my latest read). Of these, *Needful Things* is my favourite.

### The movie

I watched *Needful Things* (1993) after I bought the CD of Patrick Doyle's music. I was immediately fascinated by the main title and wanted to see the movie that inspired the composer to produce such a great soundtrack.

I do not generally like reading King's books, but I am also not a big fan of a Big Mac, and the author described his books in an interview long ago as "Big Macs". For me, King's books are often too long and too boring at the beginning, but these slow parts when King is developing the concept of the horror later are essential. The author wants his readers first to develop a relationship with the characters. Therefore, you feel touched when the horror faces them.

When reading *Pet Sematary*, I began to like the family and was shocked when the animal died. Because of the relationship, the family developed with the cat, it is understandable why the family keeps him even though his personality changed after they buried it in the pet cemetery.

Most directors make the mistake of cutting these slower parts und just concentrating on the action, but that is the wrong approach. King's books are so successful precisely because of this particular way of developing the story: the later violence depends on aspects developed in the preceding parts, and the fate of the characters touches you because you understand their feelings. A great scene to explain this approach is in the novel *Needful Things* when Leland Gaunt, who might be Satan himself, attacks Polly Chalmers, Sheriff Alan Pangborn's lover. Polly suffers from very painful arthritis, and Gaunt who has a cure for her pain attacks her verbally in an insulting manner when he offers her the cure. To receive this cure, she has to do something for him, a mean little favour, but if she does not do it, she will continue suffering. This scene is very well developed, and we begin to hate Gaunt because he is using Polly's suffering for his sadistic plans.

Most King movies are not convincing because the directors have not been able to let the audience develop an emotional connection with the characters. A few King movies have done it differently, such as David Cronenberg's *Dead Zone* (1983), for me still the best King movie with an excellent cast, *The Green Mile* (1999) with Tom Hanks, *The Shawshank Redemption* (1994, what a great movie!) and finally *Needful Things*. This book was the first novel King wrote after his rehabilitation from drugs and alcohol, and it features perhaps the most convincing antagonist in a Stephen King novel.

Leland Gaunt is a charming elderly gentleman who opens a small shop in a typical small town. It seems that Gaunt is ideally suited to any customer, but Gaunt asks his customers to do him a favour by doing some nasty things. What Gaunt, well aware of the conflicts between people, asks them to do slowly escalates until the whole town is eventually caught up in madness and violence. It is a fantastic idea!

*Needful Things*, directed by Charlton Heston's son Fraser, features Max von Sydow as Gaunt, Ed Harris as the policeman and Bonnie Bedelia, who also played Bruce Willis's wife in the first two *Die Hard* movies. I even like the final scene better than the last scene in the book, particularly the last sentences of Gaunt, such a mean guy.

**The music**

The CD consists of 17 tracks, two of which are classical songs (the famous *Ave Maria* by Franz Schubert and *Peer Gynt* composed by Edward Grieg). In the liner notes, Heston explained that he wanted to work with Doyle after listening to the opening tracks of *Dead Again*, also the first soundtrack by Doyle I listened to.

The composer explained in the liner notes that the music should reflect the "dark, ancient and evil qualities in Leland Gaunt, but that at the same time it should also capture his sardonic wit, good taste and charm."[32] Doyle developed the idea of using a choir when Gaunt's store explodes as the climax of the movie. He then thought it would be a great idea to have a more complex score with more vocals involved, and thought of a requiem mass.

With the main title *The Arrival*, one of the best tracks, Doyle introduces his haunting main theme. The instrumentation with the dominant string section at the beginning sounds unusual at first. I was immediately caught by this opening and like the track even more when the choir joins in.

Overall the soundtrack is a little repetitive, and Doyle needs most of the music to build up suspense, but there are a few very nice tracks such as *Needful Things* (great use of the piano which is playing the main theme), *Brian's Deed* ("running strings" in the first seconds) and *The Devil's Here* (the use of the choir is reminiscent of Jerry Goldsmith's *The Omen*).

My favourite track is *Art and the Minister*, a short one with a beautiful use of the famous Dies Irae theme. Dies Irae (Day of Wrath) is a Latin hymn attributed to the 13th century and best known for its use in the Roman Catholic requiem mass for the dead or as a funeral march. The Dies Irae poem describes the Day of Judgment when the brave souls will be saved and the bad souls are sent into eternal flames. There is a fine Dies Irae poem written by Ambrose Bierce:

Day of Satan's painful duty!
Earth shall vanish, hot and sooty;
So says Virtue, so says Beauty.

Ah! what terror shall be shaping
When the Judge the truth's undraping—
Cats from every bag escaping!

Now the trumpet's invocation
Calls the dead to condemnation;
All receive an invitation.

Death and Nature now are quaking,
And the late lamented, waking,
In their breezy shrouds are shaking. [...]


In *Art and the Minister*, Doyle uses the choir for a crucial scene and the piece is highly enjoyable. The choir is excellent here, in combination with pizzicato strings and a clarinet playing at the beginning before the rhythm gets faster, and the choir becomes more dominant and erupts after a few seconds. I immediately fell in love with this track when I heard it for the first time, and it is one of the tracks I have listened to so many times over the years that I have stopped counting.

There is also a funny story associated with it. When I was living and working in Shanghai for three years, I took a train ride from Nanjing to Shanghai and listened to this track. A young Chinese woman was sitting next to me and perhaps she could hear the louder parts of the track even though I was wearing my headphones. When I stopped listening, she asked me what kind of music this was. She was amazed that someone was listening to this kind of music and not to a well-known pop song. We then had a chat about the movie and the composer.  At the next station, she got off and I continued my journey. I did not even know her name and forgot to introduce myself.

*Just Blow Them Away* is the track for the surprising showdown. Screenplay author W.D. Richter (who also wrote the screenplay for John Badham's *Dracula*) changed the final scenes to a new ending. *End Titles* brings the CD to a wonderful ending. For me *Needful Things* is one of the best soundtracks by Patrick Doyle and highly enjoyable. A must-have in my opinion!

# 23. ID4 – "Welcome to earth"

*Independence Day* (1996) is one of the few scores that I know I have to put into this book. I attended the live performance of the movie on 22 September 2016 at the Royal Albert Hall in London. British composer David Arnold attended the pre-talk before the movie was shown, and entertained the audience in a very sophisticated way. We all had great fun and the *End Credits* music is one of my all-time favourite tracks.

## The movie

I posted the review of *ID4* on my website after seeing the sequel and started with some comments about it. There is no reason to repeat them here. I watched *ID 4* when I was studying in Germany and was very curious about the movie because a German director had gone to Hollywood and made one of the best disaster movies ever, according to the American press, so I wanted to see it! Of course, the "serious" German press could not find anything good in this movie and severely criticised the patriotic aspects of the film. It is funny that German directors in particular, such as Wolfgang Peterson and Roland Emmerich, have made some of Hollywood's most patriotic movies.

I really liked *ID4* when I first saw it. Even in 2016 during the live performance, you can see how fresh the movie still appears, how funny some scenes still are and how good the cast is. This movie has a great entertaining effect, some still very nice special effects, especially when the White House is blown up, and it made Will Smith a star. Emmerich claimed that he encountered difficulties when he wanted to have Will Smith as the leading actor. If you compare *ID 4* with the sequel, you will see that one of the biggest problems with the new one is that there is not such a cool actor as Will Smith in the sequel. The scene in which Smith punches the alien in the face and says the now famous quote "Welcome to Earth" is one of my all-time favourites and a classic. Fox pushed trailers showing the destruction of the White House in the presidential election year and created the effect that the audience really wants to see the movie.

## The music

David Arnold had worked with Emmerich on *Stargate* (1994) and created a lovely score with an epic main theme. Emmerich therefore hired the composer again for *ID4* and later *Godzilla* (1998), but Arnold seems to be more popular for his scores for five James Bond movies before long-term composer Thomas Newman took over with Sam Mendes as the director. In my opinion, Arnold's Bond scores are far better than Newman's. Arnold, a John Barry fan, created precisely the right and highly enjoyable mixture of orchestra and modern instruments that brought James Bond into the new century.

If you compare the music for *ID4* with the sequel, it is clear how good the original score is. Arnold composed a majestic theme that was used in the end credits of the new one, and the score won a Grammy. Arnold recorded the score with an orchestra of 90 musicians, a choir of 46 singers and "every last ounce of stereotypical Americana," producer Dean Devlin commented: "You can leave it up to a Brit to write some of the most rousing and patriotic music in the history of American cinema," said Devlin in an interview on *Filmtracks*. [33]

The soundtrack has had two official CD releases. RCA released a 50-minute album when the film came out, then in 2010 La-La Land Records released a limited edition two-CD set with the complete score plus 12 alternate cues.

My favourite is the last track, *End Credits*, a wonderful nine-minute track that uses all the themes of the score, especially the famous fanfare. This track can be played in a concert hall without any changes being made, and I was so lucky to hear this during the live performance of *ID 4*. Except for this fanfare, there are two more themes: one for the quieter moments and then the third theme for the aliens. The second theme can be heard for example in *Aftermath*, and especially in the patriotic *The President's Speech* (starting at 1'22). For Will Smith, Arnold composed a special theme that can be heard in *The Wedding* and *Cancelled Leave*.

Other highlights in the score are *First Sighting/AWAC Attack*, *The Darkest Day* - the aliens are there! – *Base Attack*, a great action piece, and of course the music for the showdown *The Launch Tunnel/Mutha Ship/Virus Uploaded*, and finally *Victory* as a more patriotic one again.

*ID4* is not only a highlight of film music in the 1990s, but one of the last really great orchestra scores in the tradition of John Williams and Jerry Goldsmith. Arnold worked with Emmerich on *Godzilla*, but for me *ID4* is Arnold's best score so far.

It seems that except for *ID4* and the James Bond movies, Arnold's music is no longer very popular. This is sad because he showed that he could create highly enjoyable music and themes to remember. Perhaps David Arnold needs a popular blockbuster again to get back into people's mind? Give it to this man, please!

# 24. THE TEN COMMANDMENTS – NEARLY A HOLY SOUND

Elmer Bernstein is one of my favourite composers. He is very well known for his score for the western *The Magnificent Seven* (1960), which I will discuss later in this book, but I wanted to introduce Bernstein with an unusual score for him: *The Ten Commandments* (1956).

I attended the Elmer Bernstein 95th birthday concert at the Royal Albert Hall in London on 18 June 2017. This concert was conducted by his son, Peter Bernstein, and director John Landis was a funny host. Elmer Bernstein seems not to be so popular among film music fans these days, even though he was nominated for 14 Oscars, both for original scores and songs. He won the Academy Award just once for *Thoroughly Modern Millie* (1967) starring Julie Andrews, just like Jerry Goldsmith was nominated many times, but only won one Academy Award.

Initially, Hollywood composer Victor Young was to compose the score for *The Ten Commandments*, but he was already too ill so he recommended Elmer Bernstein, who did an amazing job. In the concert, John Landis pointed out that the challenge in composing the music for this movie was that we do not know very much about ancient music. So this music had to be created by Elmer Bernstein and later Miklós Rózsa for *Ben Hur* with Charlton Heston.

Landis furthermore praised how gifted Bernstein was. Owing to the success of his score, he was called a master of epic scores. After the success of his jazz scores such as *The Man with the Golden Arm* (1956), Bernstein was called a master of jazz, then he was considered as a master of drama after *To Kill a Mockingbird* (1963), a master of the western after *The Magnificent Seven* (1960) and, finally, after the success of working with John Landis on comedies such as *Spies Like Us* (1985) or *Three Amigos!* (1986), a master of comedy. He also worked with Martin Scorsese on the very violent *Cape Fear* remake from 1991 by using Bernard Herrmann's score and composing for Scorsese an original score for *Age of Innocence* (1993), a fabulous waltz soundtrack. I think there is no composer who can compose music for so many different genres and yet retain his own style in the way Elmer Bernstein did. I greatly admire him for this!

## The movie

I watched *The Ten Commandments* when I was a teenager and still like it. Here Cecil B. DeMille directed a remake of his movie, and Charlton Heston played a role from these ancient times for the first time here before playing the lead in the famous *Ben Hur* (1959, directed by William Wyler). At the time of its release, *The Ten Commandments* was the most expensive movie ever made.

In 1957, the film was nominated for seven Academy Awards, including Best Picture, and won the Academy Award for Best Visual Effects by John P. Fulton. Yul Brynner won the National Board of Review Award for Best Actor for his role as Rameses, and the movie was also one of the most financially successful films ever made, grossing approximately $122.7 million at the box office during its initial release. According to Guinness World Records in terms of theatrical exhibition, it is the seventh most successful film of all time when the box office gross is adjusted for inflation.

The parting of the Red Sea was considered the most difficult special effect ever performed. This scene took about six months to film and combined scenes shot at the Red Sea in Egypt with scenes filmed at Paramount Studios of a huge water tank split a U-shaped trough, as well as the filming of a giant waterfall, also built in the studios to create the effect of the walls of the parted sea. There is so much more to discover about this movie, but let's talk about the music.

## The music

Victor Young was Cecil B. DeMille's favourite composer, but already ill, he felt that he did not have enough energy to do the score. Elmer Bernstein mentioned that Young recommended him and so did exactly what he thought DeMille would expect. The result is one of the best soundtracks ever and amazing movie music. An interesting fact is that Bernstein was better known at the time for his jazz scores. As John Landis explained in the concert, the story went round that DeMille came to Bernstein and said he liked these jazz scores, but Bernstein should not compose anything like them for his movie!

After some auditioning and interviews, DeMille asked Bernstein, "Do you think you could do for film music what Puccini did for opera?" After considering the question, the composer's reply was, "I can\t be sure -- but I would love to try."[34] I love Bernstein's honesty; he really was a great guy. Bernstein pointed out at the time: "I hope to continue to grow as a musician, but at this moment I cannot even dream of ever again obtaining as important and challenging an assignment as composing the music for *The Ten Commandments...* It was a very complex problem since the composition had to express scripture, history and drama in music. The score is composed of symphonic themes, identifying momentous events and significant personages as well as the great mass of people through whose trials and triumphs history moves. The music attempts to enhance the experience of actuality and to add to the atmosphere of authenticity. I hope that it also helps to suggest the lasting truth of the film's inspired message... Of all the arts, I strongly feel that music is closest to religion. It is hard to explain what happens in the magical moment when suddenly there is music in my heart and mind, and I can go to the piano and express it in sound. That is why I feel that music above all other arts can come closest to expressing religious experience and conveying it to others." [35]

Like Richard Wagner in his operas, Bernstein used the leitmotiv technique and created individual motifs for the most important characters. Bernstein also used some unusual instruments, mainly in the interests of authenticity. A good example of this is the Exodus sequence in which you can hear a shofar (ram's horn), symbolising the slaves' freedom after 400 years in bondage. According to Hebraic tradition, this was the instrument that heralded the Exodus from Egypt thirty-three centuries ago and is still used today.

The score is very majestic, like Miklós Rózsa's score for *Ben Hur*, but I like Bernstein's score more. It has more lyrical parts, the melodies are nicer, and the orchestration sounds more appealing to me. The *Prelude* introduces the majestic main theme. This score is unusual for Bernstein's scores, he had never written this kind of a majestic score with such a heavy emphasis on the brass section, but for this movie and its religious emotions and theatrical approach it was quite right and worked perfectly.

With *Love and Ambition*, you have a wonderful love theme, played mostly on strings. *I Am What I Am* underscores when God talks to Moses, one of the best tracks of the score. There is some similarity with Puccini or Verdi's way of creating melodramatic emotions, but what I like in this track is the use of the strings to create a kind of... yes, let's say it, atmosphere of a holy spirit, heaven and presence of God... Call it what you want, but after listening to this track, I always have this piece of music in my mind when entering a church for the first time.

*Overture* introduces the second part of the movie after the break and is a lovely piece. *The Exodus* is another highlight. Listen to the fanfares at the beginning to express the feeling that the long-awaited journey will finally start. *The Pillar of Fire* underscores the scene when Ramses starts to follow the former slaves and a wall of fire stops the Egyptians. *The Red Sea* is another highlight that underscores the scenes when the Hebrews start to enter the Red Sea.

The last two tracks are *The Ten Commandments* – when Moses receives God's rules – and then *Go, Proclaim Liberty*. This is another majestic piece of music and highly enjoyable with the percussion at the end. If you think that this soundtrack is now 60 years old, it is astonishing how timeless the music is. For me, Bernstein created not only amazing movie music with this score, but also a kind of holy sound that will come to mind when you enter a church or read episodes from the Bible.

## 25. DRACULA – A LOVE STORY

John Badham's *Dracula* (1979) is half of a good movie. If the director, author and producers had put more effort into it, it would have been the best Dracula movie ever. John Williams's score to *Dracula* is a masterpiece and with *The Fury* one of his best scores. Kevin Mulhall explains in his liner notes to the *Dracula* soundtrack that it became a "major industry status symbol for a producer or director to have John Williams and the London Symphony Orchestra signed to score their film. These were the contributing reasons which led to Williams being commissioned to score Dracula in 1978."

**The movie**

Everyone who read Bram Stokers *Dracula* gothic horror classic from 1897 is enthusiastic about the novel's great dramaturgical structure. The plot is mostly told in epistolary format, as a series of letters, diary entries, newspaper articles and ships' log entries. The narrators are the novel's protagonists. Even though Stoker's book was not the first vampire story and was perhaps influenced by Sheridan Le Fanu's novel *Carmilla* (1871) about a lesbian vampire, and perhaps also by John Polidori's tale *The Vampyre* (1819) which portrayed a vampire as an aristocrat, Stoker's novel became the ultimate vampire novel.

The book is still a great read, but it lacks an excellent showdown. Therefore, every movie tries to create a new one, but just a few have succeeded in this approach. One of the best is definitely Terence Fisher's *Dracula* from 1958. Even though Francis Ford Coppola's *Dracula* is a fine movie, he failed to create a convincing showdown by turning the ending too much into a love story, with the adaptation becoming a little bit trashy in the end.

John Badham's movie was not based on the novel. It was based on the famous Dracula actor Bela Lugosi's movie, which in turn was based on the stage play by Hamilton Deane and John L. Balderston. Frank Langella received a Tony Award nomination for his performance in the play which had a 900-show run. Even though Badham's movie is not based on the novel, it is still one of the best *Dracula* movies because Badham did not focus so much on the horror elements, but instead adapted *Dracula* into a love story.

It is interesting to note that in 1979 three major Dracula films were released simultaneously around the world: Werner Herzog's re-telling of *Nosferatu* with Klaus Kinski (not a good one), George Hamilton's *Love at First Bite*, a so-so parody of the vampire genre with a wonderful performance by Richard Benjamin as the Van Helsing character, and John Badham's *Dracula*.

W.D. Richter's adaption of the story placed a strong emphasis on the love aspects, but also caused some irritation by unnecessarily changing the names of the two female characters. Now it is Lucy who is haunted by Dracula, not Mina. There was no reason for doing this. Richter also created a new showdown that brings the story to a surprising end, and for the people who have not seen the movie, I shall say no more.

Two years previous, John Badham had directed *Saturday Night Fever* and made John Travolta a star. Perhaps because of that, some critics blamed Frank Langella's performance for being a Dracula-Travolta. For *Dracula*, Badham brought a terrific cast together: Donald Pleasance turned down the part of Van Helsing and played Dr Seward, instead Laurence Olivier played Van Helsing, and Kate Nelligan played Lucy.

Frank Langella did not show any vampire teeth during his performance and was much younger than Christopher Lee when he first played Dracula. When Lee is approaching women, you sometimes get the feeling that these women want to sleep with their father because of the age difference. Langella played Dracula as a very well-educated and elegant man with manners and a touch of tragedy, as mentioned in the dialogue with Lucy when they are having dinner at his home. He can also immediately become very brutal and violent, as can be seen at the beginning, in the killing of Renfield and in the showdown.

The movie is wonderfully photographed by Gilbert Taylor. The love scene is very romantic but also a bit trashy with its visual effects. Anyway, if you have not seen this *Dracula* movie, I highly recommend watching it, despite its structural weakness.

### The music

John Williams's music is amazing, one of his best soundtracks even though there is just one main theme. This theme is haunting, darkly melodic, gothic and beautiful. The balance between the string and the brass section in the first track of the score is indeed a sign of the tremendous composing qualities of John Williams at his best.

The score has a great many very nice tracks, and it is hard to limit myself to mentioning just a few of them. Another highlight is the second track, *To Scarborough*, a fast-moving scherzo piece with a high emphasis on the brass section. The third highlight is *The Abduction of Lucy*: here again you can hear the haunting Dracula theme in the strings section, but listen to the use of the flutes and the percussion in that track.

Finally, there is *The Love Scene*, a kind of surreal wedding scene, and if you listen carefully, you can hear one of the few musical ways of transforming a sexual orgasm into music. The last two tracks *Dracula's Death* and *End Title* bring the album to the musical climax and a satisfying ending, wonderfully played by the London Symphony Orchestra. I especially like the first seconds of the last track with the flute, before the brass and strings take over with the gothic Dracula theme.

People on Amazon criticise this album for having just one theme with the entire score composed around this theme. That is true. It is a very efficient way of composing a soundtrack, but also typical for Williams's soundtracks in general.

In the end, you have to admit that the movie is a big disappointment. It was a good chance to tell the Dracula story in a new way, but failed in this approach: too much violence, too many awkward scenes and too many trashy ones. Langella's performance is remarkable, and this and John Williams's music are responsible for the movie still not being forgotten.

## 26. EDWARD SCISSORHANDS – A MODERN FAIRY TALE

Before Hans Zimmer entered the film music scene, Danny Elfman was the guy who composed the music for Superhero movies such as *Batman* (1989) or *Spider-Man* (2002). Elfman has had a long and successful collaboration with director Tim Burton, and both have been responsible for some great movies such as *Beetlejuice* (1988), *Batman* (1989), *Edward Scissorhands* (1990), *Batman Returns* (1992), *The Nightmare Before Christmas* (1993), *Mars Attacks!* (1996), *Sleepy Hollow* (1999), *Planet Of The Apes* (2001), *Big Fish* (2003), *Corpse Bride* (2005) and *Big Eyes* (2014), and these are not even all the movies that Burton and Elfman have worked on together.

Furthermore, Elfman composed the title music for the TV series *The Simpsons* and *Desperate Housewives*, the *Men In Black* movies (1997–2002), *Fifty Shades of Grey* (2015) and many more. Elfman's style is mostly minimalistic, easy to recognise because of the special orchestration and fun to listen to. One of my first soundtracks by Elfman was *Edward Scissorhands*, and because this soundtrack is very typical for Elfman and was a huge success, I have decided to introduce Elfman in my book with this one.

### The movie

*Edward Scissorhands* was one of the first Tim Burton movies I watched. As a big fan of American horror star Vincent Price, I was very curious about this movie and considered the plot to be a mixture of romantic, scary and haunting all together, like a magnificent fairy tale. Tim Burton developed the idea before his *Batman* movie, but was only able to finally make it after the huge success he had with *Batman*.

I read that Tom Cruise was the studio's preferred choice for the lead, but the meeting with Cruise and Burton was not successful. Even Tom Hanks turned the part down, so it finally went to Johnny Depp, Burton's first choice. Depp "wept like a newborn" and immediately found personal and emotional connections with the story. Stan Winston created the scissor hands for Edward, and the role of the inventor was explicitly developed for Vincent Price, his last role before he died.

It is also interesting to know that the genesis of "Edward" came from a drawing by Burton as a teenager, which reflected his feelings of isolation and being unable to communicate with the people around him in his home town of Burbank. Caroline Thompson, a young novelist, translated Burton's idea into a screenplay.

The movie is one of the most fabulous fairy tales Burton has ever put on screen. Edward is found living alone in the attic of a Gothic castle, a setting that is also used for the main characters in *Batman* and *The Nightmare Before Christmas*. As in Mary Shelley's *Frankenstein*, a mob confronts the "evil creature" and tries to kill him. Like *Beauty and the Beast*, Edward is unable to express his affection for the woman he loves, in the movie the female character is named Kim, played by first-choice actress Winona Ryder. Last but not least, in its setting and topics, the film shows the considerable influence of German Expressionism and Gothic fiction archetypes.

I want to close my comments about the movie with just a small observation: when you watch the beginning and end scenes and see this little girl in her huge bed, you can imagine how clever Tim Burton is at giving his audience a vision of how lonely a child can sometimes feel in his or her bed...

## The music

*Edward Scissorhands* was the fourth feature film collaboration between director Burton and composer Elfman. The orchestra consisted of 79 musicians, and Elfman considered *Scissorhands* to be his most personal and favourite work. In addition to Elfman's music, three Tom Jones songs were also added. The main theme became one of Elfman's best-known themes. When I attended a Jerry Goldsmith concert in London, I met a local jazz composer who was writing the music for a Christmas movie from Albania. The director had asked him to compose the music exactly in the style of *Edward Scissorhands*.

For me, *Batman* and *Edward Scissorhands* are Elfman's best scores. Both were orchestrated by Steve Bartek and conducted by Shirley Walker. Elfman used his typical minimalistic style but also added a choir to increase the lyrical approach. Furthermore, the choir emphasised the fairy tale aspects. The main theme is a beautiful waltz, and Elfman starts with some chimes so the music sounds like a lullaby.

The album from 1990 has 16 score tracks and runs 49 minutes. Like all Elfman scores, the music becomes a little bit repetitive after a while. You can skip some tracks and listen to the best ones. One of these is for one of the most beautiful scenes in the movie: "Ice Dance": During the Christmas holiday, Edward carves an angel ice sculpture modelled after Kim. The ice shavings being thrown into the air and falling like snow, a rarity in this town which is mostly hot and warm. Kim is excited about the beauty of this snow and begins to dance in the snowfall. Jim, Kim's jealous boyfriend, arrives and calls out to Edward, which surprises him, and so he accidentally cuts Kim's hand.

The album is musical storytelling at his best: after with *Introduction* the lovely main theme is introduced and then track 2 *Storytelling* gives us the background to the story we will see. Elfman composed a lovely piece with track 3 *Castle On The Hills*, suggesting the haunting and darker aspects of the story and the score start. Track 4 *Beautiful New World/Home Sweet Home* has a wonderful opening when Elfman uses a harp. Track 5 *Cookie Factory* is one of the tracks I normally skip; it is composed in the typical *Beetlejuice* style. I am not a big fan of this kind of music so I also skip the next track *Ballet De Suburbia* (even though the use of the sax is very nice). These tracks are more musical Micky Mousing, which Elfman is really good at.

We then have the *Ice Dance*, and with *Edward Meets the World: Etiquette Lesson* we are back to the lyrical parts. *Edward the Barber* is more of a musical joke with a funny use of Spanish castanets and a nice fast woodwind performance. The following track, *Esmeralda*, is a short one, and then *Death* gives us one of the saddest tracks, a good musical expression of loneliness. *The Tide Turns* comprise three key scenes: the House Robbery, Kevin's Rescue, and Edward's Outburst. I also normally skip this one.

In *Final Confrontation*, we have the dramatic music for the showdown. Elfman uses the choir in a very haunting way. The music is purely dramatic and definitely one of the best tracks Elfman ever composed. Even though the scene is very dramatic, Elfman balances the track very well between the lyrical parts and the dramatic moments. You should listen to the next tracks *Farewell*, *The Grand Finale* and *The End* together without taking a break. This works as a wonderful suite, with *The Grand Finale* one of the best tracks of the whole score.

*Edward Scissorhands* is not only a wonderful score, but is definitely also one of the best scores Elfman ever composed – a heart-warming score that can bring tears to the eyes. *Edward Scissorhands* is one of the few examples of a terrific story and a score that matches it!

## 27. Psycho – The ultimate horror score

I decided to put *Psycho* after talking about Danny Elfman because when Elfman entered the music scene, some people compared him to Bernhard Herrmann. The dark and romantic atmosphere of Elfman's scores seems to be similar to Herrmann's therefore Elfman was hired to create the music for the unnecessary *Psycho* remake by Gus Van Sant and also for *Hitchcock* (2012), the Hitchcock biopic by Sacha Gervasi about preparations for and the shooting of *Psycho*. Anthony Hopkins gave a very nice performance as Alfred Hitchcock.

If you look closer at the Elfman's and Herrmann's scores, there are not many similarities. Herrmann was a master at dealing with the orchestra, both for suspense and romantic music. Elfman's musical style is more minimalistic, often like a lullaby, very suitable for darker movies, but his scores are not as sophisticatedly orchestrated as Herrmann's and are much simpler in the composing style. This is not meant as a criticism, just an observation.

### The movie

*Psycho* (1960) is a masterpiece: it was the first slasher movie in history and totally shocked the audience in numerous ways. The shower murder scene still holds the record as the most discussed movie music scene, and Bernard Herrmann's score is considered the ultimate score for a horror movie. There is so much to say about this movie and the music that it is difficult to condense it down to just two pages.

American writer Robert Bloch (1917-1994) is one of the best writers of crime and horror novels and short stories. He had a wicked sense of humour, and his short stories are famous for the surprising twists at the end. Bloch is reported to have once said: "I have the heart of a child, it stands in a glass bottle on my desk" to explain his unusual sense of twists. He started out writing for pulp magazines such as *Weird Tales* and was influenced by H. P. Lovecraft (1890-1937), the American horror story writer who became famous as the creator of the *Cthulhu Mythos*. Bloch and Lovecraft developed a friendship by writing letters, and both killed each other in short stories: as I said a wicked sense of humour.

In 1959 Bloch wrote *Psycho*, a novel about a serial killer with a split personality, based on the real serial killer Ed Gein who also was an inspiration for *The Silence of the Lambs* (1991). Bloch, however, commented that it was the situation itself – a mass murderer living undetected in a small town in middle America – rather than Gein himself that inspired his storyline. I read the book 30 years ago for the first time, and even though Bloch is one of my favourite writers of crime novels, this novel is not his best. Two aspects were responsible for *Psycho* working very well: the shocking killing of Marion, the main character until her death, and the identity of Norman.

Bloch was not aware of who really bought the rights for the movie adaption so Hitchcock was able to agree a great deal. The sequel to Hitchcock's movie *Psycho 2* (1983) is poor, even though it has some good scenes. I also think that Jerry Goldsmith's score is one of his weakest, but Bloch's own sequel *Psycho 2* is also a bad novel. And the worst idea ever was Gus Van Sant's "shot-by-shot" remake. He added two scenes – a spider crawling out of Mrs Bates mouth, and Norman masturbating when seeing Marion – both rubbish ideas and, like the complete remake, just a waste of time.

Even though Alfred Hitchcock created a masterpiece with *Psycho*, the critics at that time did not like the movie. But the critics were never fair to Hitchcock. The movie was a huge box office success, also because of Hitch's very clever marketing idea: the "no late admission" policy for the film was unusual for the time and made the audience curious about the movie.

The shower murder scene is the most famous scene. A lot of myths exist about this scene. For example, graphic designer Saul Bass claimed that he directed the scene. Janet Leigh denied this in an interview and said that Hitchcock was directing this scene, and no body double was used. The scene was shot in December 1959 with 77 different camera angles. It is fascinating that the whole scene is working mostly in the mind of the audience because there is no close up of the knife hitting Marion's body. I am not a big fan of the psychological analysis of this scene and personally do not care if the knife is a symbol of a penis or whether this murder scene is meant to be a rape scene. It is a gorgeous scene and proof that Hitchcock is perhaps the best director of crime movies ever.

**The music**

Bernard Herrmann was the composer for a lot of Hitchcock movies, and with *Psycho* he created his masterpiece. You can see the importance of Herrmann's contribution to the film in the opening credit sequence when the name of the composer is only followed by Alfred Hitchcock's directing credit. Herrmann took the reduced music budget to compose a score just for strings and not for a full orchestra. The strings are also a reference to the black-and-white shooting of the film and create a darker and very intense effect.

The use of the strings is significant in another way. As can be read in the liner notes by Christopher Palmer to the release of the complete score of *Psycho*, strings were mostly associated with romance. In nine out of ten romantic scenes, the violins will underscore and emphasise the emotions of that scene. In a modern symphony orchestra, the strings are normally the largest section and because of their "basic single tone-colour" can "command a great number and variety of special effects: pizzicato, tremolando, harmonics and so on". [36]

The main title music is a very tense and hurtling piece. Palmer describes it as "fast, urgent, nervous"[37]. It is not a melody; it is more a rhythm than a theme, a hunting, forward-driving and hammering rhythm that you cannot get out of your head once you have heard it. After the prelude music, you have a kind of love theme, but the overall *Psycho* motif is so strong that you can feel there will be not much love in this movie. With the end of the scene, you can feel that the relationship between Marion and Sam is over until Marion makes the decision to escape, with the money, and is hunted by the *Psycho* motif during the following scenes

A very good main title music normally sets the tone for the whole movie, and in combination with the title sequence created by Saul Bass, you can imagine the kind of violence that is coming. The *Psycho* rhythm anticipates fear, panic, chase and hunting. Even though there is no murder or any shocking sequence for the first 20 minutes, the audience can feel the tension of the plot just because of this dramatic music.

The music for the shower scene is very famous. Herrmann used the strings and the unique way they were played to transform the shocking violence into music. Try to watch the scene without the music, and then you can understand the genius of Herrmann's approach. Music critics recognise a similarity between the sound of the music and Norman Bates's hobby for birds, but I do not think this idea makes any sense. Herrmann just tried to use the best effect to scare the hell out of the audience. The music is often described as "bird-shrieks or distorted screaming bird-cries."[38]

Why birds? Because Norman likes to stuff birds, as he explained to Marion in the dinner scene. The shrieking effect is created by reiterated, dissonant, sharp downbow strokes and wild glissandos: a brutal harshness by using the extreme top register of each instrument. Herrmann was asked what he had in mind when composing for that scene, and he replied with one word: "Terror."

It is also interesting that Hitchcock initially did not want to have music in this scene, but was convinced when Herrmann played the cue. Herrmann biographer Steven C. Smith wrote: "When Herrmann played the shower scene cue, the director approved its use. Herrmann reminded Hitchcock of his instructions not to score this scene, to which Hitchcock replied, 'Improper suggestion, my boy, improper suggestion.'"[39] A survey conducted by PRS for Music in 2009 showed that the British public considers the score from "the shower scene" to be the scariest theme in any film.

There is so much to say about the movie and the music, but let's stop it here. You can also analyse a movie and a soundtrack to death. Let me give you one recommendation: I found a great music clip on YouTube called *Psycho with Knives*. Even though I did not like the middle part of this track (the artist is improvising on the main theme, so no original Bernhard Herrmann music), the idea using the knives on the piano and including this into the music is just a great idea and makes it a lot of fun to listen to.

The final music for the famous last scene of *Psycho* is described by Palmer as a "chord without a resolution, a finale without an ending"[40], and here you can see how modern Bernard Herrmann's music still is. *Psycho* is a film with an open ending – what will happen to Norman? – and Herrmann's music does not give us the final resolution either than previous film music scores have. Furthermore, after hearing *Psycho*, it is impossible to listen to romantic string melodies without having the *Psycho* score in mind. So is it possible to say that *Psycho* is not only the ultimate horror music, but also the score that destroyed the romantic movie music genre?

## 28. FOR YOUR EYES ONLY – ROCKY MEETS BOND

Another Bill Conti score, this time the James Bond soundtrack for *For Your Eyes Only* (1981). Some fans think that the song is the best James Bond song ever. Even though Sheena Easton gives a great performance, I like the Shirley Bassey songs more, but I am also a big fan of a-ha's *The Living Daylights*. Try to compare their version with the final arrangement in the movie and listen to the different orchestration.

**The movie**

*For Your Eyes Only* is the result of a new approach in the James Bond era. *Moonraker*, the first and only James Bond discussed here so far, is great fun, but some critics and fans think that the movie was too over the top: too many gadgets, too many silly jokes and too much SF. Bond movies were getting bigger and bigger, but it seems they were not as much fun as the earlier movies. Compare *Moonraker* with Connery's best James Bond *From Russia with Love*, and you know what I mean.

So, *For Your Eyes Only* took a more serious approach. Director Lewis Gilbert and screenplay author Christopher Wood were not hired again; instead Richard Maibaum and Michael G. Wilson – step-son of James Bond producer Albert R. Broccoli – took over, but Roger Moore still played James Bond even though screenings with other actors were done in parallel because it was unknown whether Moore wanted to play the role again.

Former cutter John Glen was hired as director, the gadgets were reduced to a minimum – Glen pointed out he wanted to show this severe new approach in the scene in which the Lotus is blown up by itself – the humour was still there, as was typical for the Roger Moore era, but the movie was now very realistic and had an unusually strong narrative theme of revenge. Here it works much better than in Timothy Dalton's second and last James Bond movie *Licence to Kill* (1989, also John Glen's last James Bond movie and because of the high amount of violence nicknamed "Rambo-Bond" or Rambond"). In *For Your Eyes Only*, the action scenes are not over the top and are sometimes shockingly brutal, especially the murder of Melina's parents. In one scene, Bond is acting like a killer when he gives a bad guy in his car the final kick so that the car goes over the cliff. This manner of cold-blooded killing is reminiscent of the scene in which Sean Connery kills Prof Dent (Anthony Dawson) and uses his new Walther PPK gun for the first time.

The movie got and still receives mixed reviews. Some fans like it because of the serious approach and its return to greater credibility, but do not like the silly final scene with the parody of Margaret Thatcher, the only stupid joke in the whole movie. The stunts were praised, with the ski stunts in particular being famous. The pre-title sequence with Bond finally killing Blofeld is an exciting start for the film, but a silly ending for this tremendous antagonist that Bond had fought three times. You have wished a better death for Blofeld; this is just a silly one.

## The music

*For Your Eyes Only* is not my favourite James Bond movie – I still like *Moonraker, The Spy Who Loved Me, From Russia with Love, On Her Majesty's Secret Service* and Daniel Craig's *Casino Royale* more – but let's discuss the music because Bill Conti's contribution to the franchise is one of the best soundtracks in his career and one of the best Bond soundtracks.

In an interview with Emmy TV Legends, Bill Conti explained that John Barry was not able to do the movie and so recommended him. Conti was happy about the opportunity and mentioned that Bond producer "Cubby" Broccoli invited him, his wife and his two daughters to England for three months so that Conti could write *For Your Eyes Only*.

Conti wanted Barbra Streisand to write the lyrics and Donna Summer to sing it, but the studio suggested Sheena Easton. Conti was impressed when he listened to her singing because she was a terrific singer. Conti also explained that Michael Leeson who wrote the lyrics had created a fantastic ending line for the song, but title designer Maurice Binder wanted to start the song with the title *For Your Eyes Only* and therefore, when you see the title of the movie, the lyrics start with the main line "For Your Eyes Only". Singer Sheena Easton was also the first singer in Bond history to appear on screen.

Conti added to the usual Bond sound, which generally focused heavily on the brass section, his individual composing style and a lot of contemporary disco elements and synthesisers. His sense of melodies and dramatic atmosphere can be heard throughout the soundtrack. Even though *Submarine* is not one of the best parts of the score, I highly appreciate Conti's sense for building up suspense in this underwater scene.

A *Drive in the Country* is a highly enjoyable piece during the famous car chase with the 2CV. The composing style is typical 80s, but also typical Conti. *Gonzales takes a drive* starts with some Mexican music and then switches after Gonzales's murder to typical 80s action music. I am not a big fan of this second part of that track. Another track to skip is *Ski... Shoot... Jump*, just suspense music. Typical of the *For Your Eyes Only* score is that you have excellent music, but also very weak tracks like the ones I just mentioned.

*St. Cyril's Monastery* and *Run Them Down/The Climb* are played when Bond is climbing up to Kristatos's place for the showdown. Both tracks are very good, and you can experience again how Conti builds the atmosphere, especially when 007 starts to climb. Conti even transformed the elevator's ascent into music. The last twenty seconds of *Run Them Down* are very nice: Conti uses the strings first to build up suspense, and then the percussion comes in before the track suddenly ends. These few seconds are just one reason to buy the music.

There is also a nice instrumental version of the title song. Conti uses a trumpet instead of the vocals. When I was attending one of the James Bond concerts in London, the conductor told us that Derek Watkins, the British trumpet player who played on every James Bond film soundtrack apart from *Skyfall*, had died aged 68[41]. *The P.M. Gets the Bird/For Your Eyes Only* (the music for the childish Thatcher scene) was the last track on the first release of the soundtrack album but the extended edition ends with *Run Them Down...*

My favourite track is *Runaway*, the music composed for the famous ski chase in the movie. Unfortunately, one stuntman died during filming. Even today, this action scene is amazing and one of the best in the Bond franchise. *Runaway*, in my opinion not played loudly enough in the movie, is an excellent action track. Conti at his best!

By listening to how Conti uses the brass, the strings and the percussion, you can hear how gifted this composer is. Listen to the part of the music when

Bond runs over the table – the music slows down here a little before getting back into the action.

Of course, John Barry is THE composer of James Bond music, but Bill Conti did a tremendous job and added fresh ideas to the music. For me, the music is the best part of the movie. After John Barry resigned as Bond composer, David Arnold did a great job with his scores, but Bill Conti's still stands out as the best non-John Barry James Bond score.

# 29. The Final Countdown – The 70s Top Gun

This will be the only review of a soundtrack by John Scott in my book. I have two scores in my collection, *The Final Countdown* and his music to Jean-Claude van Damme's *Lionheart* (1990). I like the music for *The Final Countdown*, and musically it is a better score than *Lionheart*, so I have decided to put this review in my book. The main theme is such a great example of amazing movie music that if you do not have the soundtrack, get the CD and listen to this musical expression of flying in the air.

## The composer

John Scott is an English film composer who has collaborated with directors such as Richard Donner, Norman Jewison, Irvin Kershner and many others and is well known for his collaboration with the French explorer Jacques Cousteau on his documentaries.

He also composed a score for *The Prayer for the Dying* (1987), the Mike Hodges drama about a former IRA member. The score was rejected, and Bill Conti composed the final score. Scott also composed the music for Roger Spottiswoode's mountain thriller *Shoot to Kill* (1988).

At the age of 14, Scott enrolled in the British Army as a boy musician and continued his musical studies of the clarinet, harp and saxophone. Later he toured with some of the best-known British bands, was hired by EMI to arrange and conduct some of its most popular artists, and worked with Beatles producer George Martin. Scott, credited as Johnny Scott, led a jazz combo during the 1960s.

Two other interesting facts to mention are that Scott played for Henry Mancini and was the principal saxophonist in John Barry's soundtrack for *Goldfinger*. Scott has composed for more than 100 film and television productions and is also active as a classical composer (having written a symphony, a ballet, four string quartets and a guitar concerto) and as a conductor. Orchestras that he has conducted include the London Philharmonic Orchestra, the London Symphony Orchestra, the Royal Philharmonic Orchestra, the Munich Symphony Orchestra, the Berlin Radio Symphony Orchestra, the Budapest Opera Orchestra, the Lubliana Radio

Orchestra and the Prague Philharmonic.

## The movie

*The Final Countdown* was the *Top Gun* of the 70s. Kirk Douglas's son Peter was the driving force behind the picture[42] and was able to get the cooperation of the United States Navy. Therefore, the film was filmed on board the USS Nimitz supercarrier. Many of the crew members of Nimitz were used as extras, a few with speaking parts. A total of 48 of the crew appear as "actors" in the final credits. The difficulties in filming a modern jet fighter were soon apparent when the first setup to record a F-14 take off at Naval Station Norfolk, Virginia, resulted in both camera and operator being pitched down a runway.

The basic idea of the script is fascinating: due to getting into a strange storm-like vortex, the Nimitz with Captain Douglas is taken back to 6 December 1941, one day before the attack on Pearl Harbour.

So now they are facing an unusual situation: should the modern aircraft strike against the incoming Japanese forces or should they do nothing because they have no idea what will happen to the time continuum if they change history, as explained by a defence expert played by Martin Sheen?

The finale of the movie lacks a really good idea for resolving this issue, but the picture is worth seeing nevertheless. Director Don Taylor also directed the sequel to *The Omen* titled *Damien: Omen II* (1978).

## The music

Except for the excellent aircraft scenes, John Scott's music is the best part of the movie. The composer took the whole project very seriously in his musical approach. You can find great music for the flying scenes and an appealing love theme with a quite impressive orchestrated approach. Owing to the music's military aspect, the score is dominated by the brass section and the percussion.

The main theme is powerful and majestic with a sublime melody. In combination with the jets in the movie and the blue sky, this theme takes the emotion of the audience with it into the sky.

The soundtrack album has 23 tracks, but when listening to the score I skip most of them. Some are too dependent on the movie. For example, for the scenes when the Vortex appears and the time warp scenes, the music sounds "frightened" to build up suspense. In the movie, the music would have worked significantly because it is a musical expression of time travel, but director Don Taylor decided just to use sound effects.

Among these tracks in the middle of the album, track 14 *Lauren and Owen* presents the love theme in a wonderfully orchestrated version. Track 17 *General Quarters* is a powerful piece of music that is perhaps reminiscent of similar tracks from Ron Goodwin's *When Eagles Dare* (1968). Track 19 *The Storm Reappears* brings the suspense back to the music before the next four tracks bring the movie to an end.

John Scott also had the chance to compose music for the end credits – a highly enjoyable track! Of course, this movie and the scenes to the end credits promote the US army. Wouldn't it be nice to become a pilot, the scenes seem to say.

Overall, John Scott did a fantastic job and the score is another excellent example of amazing movie music: timeless in its approach, using the full force of the orchestra and adding some nice unusual musical effects. I immediately liked the main theme, and on YouTube there is a clip of John Scott directing a live performance of it.

I also think that because of Scott's superb score, a lot of soundtrack fans still choose to watch this movie. If you do not have this score in your soundtrack collection, I highly recommend buying it. Enjoy this music, which is far better than the pop song compilation of Tom Cruise's *Top Gun*.

# 30. BACKDRAFT – FIGHTING FIRES IN CHICAGO

*Backdraft* (1991) was the first Hans Zimmer CD I bought and it is still one of my favourite scores. I am not sure if it is Shirley Walker's orchestration, but in my opinion this music is a much better way of underscoring action scenes than the overblown sound Hans Zimmer has developed recently with his strong focus on electronics. The last track of this score is one of my favourite Hans Zimmer tracks, and I sometimes listen to it while travelling or starting my day. The rhythm gets you going.

## The movie

*Backdraft* is an action-thriller directed by Ron Howard from 1991 about a group of firefighters in Chicago. Grossing a total of over $ 152 million, this movie is the highest grossing film ever made about firefighters. Furthermore, the movie received three Academy Award nominations, and Hans Zimmer won the BMI Film Music Award for his music.

The story about two brothers, played by William Baldwin and Kurt Russell, is not very well developed and the love story is poor because it is unnecessary. Additional, remarkable appearances are made by Robert De Niro, Donald Sutherland in some great scenes, and Scott Glen. The very realistic fire scenes are the star of the movie and on a big screen this movie is still breath-taking.

Firefighting professionals have mentioned that the fire in the film is close to reality; more realism would have resulted in the visuals in almost every fire scene being completely obscured by the smoke, with the audience having trouble seeing the actors or following the action.

The idea that the fire is acting like a living entity is also not very realistic, but precisely this idea gives the film its exceptional and demonic touch. When I visited Universal Studios years ago in Los Angeles, they had a special effects demonstration based on this movie, and you could feel the heat of the fire.

## The music

Before being appointed to compose the music for *Backdraft*, Hans Zimmer had already scored a lot of film scores and was well known for this contribution to *Rain Man* (1988) with Tom Cruise and Dustin Hoffman, Ridley Scott's *Black Rain* (1989), and in particular for his lovely score for *Driving Miss Daisy* (1989, also in my book). Zimmer's musical approach for *Backdraft* features a good mix of electronics, orchestra and choir, held together with a very majestic main theme.

Looking back at Hans Zimmer's career, I prefer the soundtracks from the 1990s. Back then, Zimmer tried to compose various soundtracks in different styles and created lovely melodies such as the theme for *Driving Miss Daisy* or *Rain Man*. In *Backdraft*, Zimmer transformed even the characteristics of this *Backdraft* fire into music.

A backdraft is an explosive event caused by a fire resulting from the rapid re-introduction of oxygen in an oxygen-depleted environment, for example caused by a window being broken or a door to an enclosed space being opened. The film shows the dangers of this backdraft for firefighters in spectacular scenes.

On Filmtracks[43], you can read that Hans Zimmer and Ron Howard, who had previously developed a strong collaboration with James Horner, did not work very well at the beginning because of miscommunication. Zimmer nearly got fired during the project. The idea of composing an "ode to firemen" was ultimately achieved by Zimmer's final approach. For this, the composer used a 95-person orchestra with a massive emphasis on the brass and percussion sections (dominance of the snare drums) and at times a female choir, especially in the action scenes.

The first track *Fighting 17th* sets the tone for the whole soundtrack. It is a slow and majestic start that introduces the main theme. The second track, *Brothers*, presents the love theme that is similar to the love theme later in *Pearl Harbor* (2001), a track that also introduces the sound effects that underscore the fire scenes because this scene is shot in a parallel storytelling about the two brothers: one has sex, the other fights the fire. Track 3 *The Arsonist's Waltz* introduces a nice waltz approach to the music, a kind of love scene, before the action starts with the next track *333*.

Track 6 *Burn It All* is a now famous action track for the firefighting scenes that introduces the special Hans Zimmer approach to underscoring action tracks. This highly effective music drives the action forward, no matter how loud the sound effects are. The female choir works very well here. A great idea: men are fighting a fire and Hans Zimmer uses a female choir to underscore this!

The action continues with the melodramatic *You Go, We Go*. Zimmer also transforms the hammering of an axe into music, like Jerry Goldsmith in *Hoosiers / Best Shot* (1986) does with the dropping of a basketball. The penultimate track called *Fahrenheit 451* – the title refers to the temperature 451 °F (233 °C) that was thought to be the auto-ignition temperature of paper; scientists now believe it is 440 °F to 470 °F – is another fabulous action track.

The second part of this track underscores the funeral. The solo trumpet also heard in the first track *Fighting 17th* gives the track the necessary majestic and patriotic tone. In the Milan CD I have, there is no break between *You Go, We Go* and *Fahrenheit 451* – these tracks belong together.

The Milan CD is not perfect, the sound quality is occasionally not that good, and the cues are different from those used in the movie. Nevertheless, *Backdraft* is a great movie music CD, very visual on the one hand but also independent of the movie.

The last track in particular, *Show me your Firetruck* is a beautiful piece of music and one of my all-time favourites. Great job, Hans! Why not compose more in that style again?

# 31. JURASSIC WORLD – A NEW BEGINNING

I will be discussing two soundtracks by Michael Giacchino in my book, the first also being the first CD I bought by this composer. Giacchino's success in the movie music business is good news because before he became successful with his scores and way of composing for a large orchestra, the movie music scene was in danger of becoming slightly boring because all the superhero movies were mostly being done by Hans Zimmer and his co-composers.

Film music should be characterised by variety, so I am glad that Giacchino is now another composer working in this field. He recently composed the music for the new *Star Trek* franchise, for *Star Wars: Rogue One* (2016), *Doctor Strange* (the same year) and the new *Spider-Man: Homecoming* (2017) and *War of the Planet of the Apes* (2017).

## The composer

Born in New Jersey, as a teenager Giacchino created short animation movies and began combining these movies with soundtracks. One of his teachers suggested to Giacchino's parents that their son should attend the School of Visual Arts in New York City. Giacchino loved the freedom at that school. He got an unpaid internship at Universal and filled this position at night while attending school during the day and also working at Macy's to pay his rent.

In 1990 Giacchino graduated with a Bachelor of Fine Arts. He later moved to Disney and got his first jobs composing music for video games. His first major composition was the music for DreamWorks' *The Lost World* video game (1997). It is interesting to note that this game was also the first to be recorded with an original live orchestral score. I am sure Giacchino never thought at that time that he would be composing the music for a *Jurassic Park* feature movie years later.

Giacchino became popular for composing music for games such as *Medal of Honor* (1999) and *Call of Duty* (2003). In 2001, J. J. Abrams hired Giacchino to compose the music for the TV series *Alias* (2001, with Jennifer Garner) and later for *Lost* (2004). Brad Bird hired the composer for Pixar's *The Incredibles* (2004), his first feature movie score and nominated for a

Grammy.

Giacchino also scored Pixar's *Up* (2009) and won the Academy Award for Best Original Score just five years after he started composing for the cinema. In 2009 Giacchino composed the music for the first movie of the new *Star Trek* franchise and created a new theme.

I have never watched *Alias* or *Lost* and have no idea why I was just not interested in these two series at that time, even though my friends were big fans of *Lost*. I just thought it was too late after two seasons to step in and I am also not a big fan of video games, so the first time I became aware of Michael Giacchino was for his music for *Ratatouille* (2007).

In my opinion, it is one of the best animation movies in recent years and this score was the first soundtrack by Giacchino I bought. I love its music, especially Giacchino's ability to write wonderful melodies combined with typical French music. The music for the end credits is wonderful. My initial idea was to introduce Giacchino in my book with this score, but then *Jurassic World* (2015) came out and I like this score more than *Ratatouille* so that is what I will be talking about.

## The movie

I watched *Jurassic World* when I was in Boston attending a summit at my business school. My first idea that Sunday evening was to listen to some live jazz music, but I could not find the right place in Boston, so I decided to watch this movie instead. During the very entertaining film, I recognised the music in a lot of scenes and really liked it. I did not know that Giacchino was behind the music and just saw his name at the end of the movie.

The score is an excellent mixture of lovely music that focuses more on atmosphere and outstanding action music. Giacchino uses John William's majestic theme from the original movie in various scenes and said in an interview on Collider.com: "It was a really targeted approach as to where to include Williams' theme and where would make the most sense and where would we most appreciate it as fans ourselves." [44]

Because of the action-packed scenes, action cues are a big part of the soundtrack, starting with track 5 *Clearly His First Rodeo*. Then we have a break with quieter tracks, but the action begins to dominate the album. The action comes back with track 10 *Fits and Jumpstarts*. I really like the first part of the track and how Giacchino creates atmosphere and suspense. The piano part with the lovely melody is very nice to listen to.

There are a lot of noisy and quite impressive orchestrated parts, and therefore overall this is not an easy listening soundtrack at all. Giacchino transforms the danger and brutality of the dinosaur attacks into music. Examples are track 12 *Love in the Time of Pterosauria*, track 13 *Chasing the Dragons* (a highlight of the score), track 14 *Raptor Your Heart Out* (great title, Giacchino is well-known among his friends for creating funny track titles), track 15 *Costa Rican Standoff* (great beginning with the percussion and the brass section) and, of course, track 16 *Our Rex is Bigger Than Yours* (nice choir at the beginning, but I do not like the use of the choir in the second part of this track because in my opinion it is a little over the top).

The action tracks overall are composed with a high amount of string movements and percussions, with the brass section sometimes interrupting with "shocking" outbursts. Track 20 is called *Jurassic World Suite* (nearly 13 min long). I am not sure what the reason was for this track, but I can remember that some of this music was used for the end credits.

Overall, I prefer the quieter parts of the score. If you think about the high number of action tracks, I sometimes have the feeling that Giacchino's composing style is a little bit too complicated. The tracks are brilliantly composed, wonderfully orchestrated and astonishingly played, but I sometimes just miss a straightforward action track like the ones by Jerry Goldsmith or John Williams.

# 32. TOTAL RECALL – JERRY GOLDSMITH'S BRUCKNER SYMPHONY

Composer Jerry Goldsmith and Dutch-born director Paul Verhoeven worked on three films together: *Total Recall* (1990), *Basic Instinct* (1992) and *Hollow Man* (2000), and from their first movie together their collaboration was highly praised. I have therefore decided to talk in my book about *Total Recall* and will close it with a review of *Basic Instinct*.

*Total Recall* (1990), the original one with Arnold Schwarzenegger and not the lousy remake with Colin Farrell and Kate Beckinsale, is one hell of a movie and one of the best action movies ever. It finally established Verhoeven, after his success with *RoboCop* (1987), as one of the most creative directors of straight-forward action movies, gave Schwarzenegger one of his most popular roles and in direct comparison with Sylvester Stallone's *Rambo III* (1988, with another Jerry Goldsmith score) showed how an intelligent action movie should be made.

It is clear how important *Total Recall* still is for Arnold Schwarzenegger because he named his autobiography *Total Recall*. The reviews of *Backdraft*, *Jurassic World*, *Total Recall*, *Jaws* and *Batman* offer five reviews of five different action scores by five different composers in my book in a row.

## The movie

I remember this movie very well because it was one of the first Arnold Schwarzenegger movies I saw at the cinema. At that time in my life, I was not such a big fan of Arnie, I preferred Sylvester Stallone with his *Rocky* series and liked the first *First Blood* movie very much, and not only because of Jerry Goldsmith's music.

Therefore, the decision to watch *Total Recall* was firstly driven by the fact that Jerry Goldsmith composed the music and Paul Verhoeven was the director. I had received the music CD a few days previously but had some trouble with the heavily action-packed score. The music sounded repetitive, even violent in musical terms, was highly-action driven and not very lyrical, but nevertheless very enjoyable.

I immediately fell in love with *The Dream* and the action track *End of a Dream*. At the same time, I also received the music to *Gremlins 2* (1990), a score I liked more than *Total Recall* because it was more fun to listen to, and I like the musical gimmicks a lot.

Looking back at *Total Recall* today, it could be argued that this might be Arnie's best movie other than *Terminator*. Critics compared *Total Recall* with *Rambo III* and said that people should go and see Schwarzenegger's movie because it was worth every dollar spent on the ticket, it was a lot of fun and the audience would be greatly entertained.

In my memory, this movie is also the first time I preferred a Schwarzenegger movie to a Stallone movie, and I then began following Schwarzenegger's career and admired the way he became Governor of California.

Based on the story *We Can Remember It for You Wholesale* by the famous SF writer Philip K. Dick, a still enjoyable read, *Alien* writers Dan O'Bannon and Ronald Shusett wrote a screenplay, but it was passed from studio to studio. Finally, Dino De Laurentiis took on the project. The Italian producer, who also produced Schwarzenegger's first hit movie *Conan The Barbarian* (1982, with a fabulous score by Basil Poledouris which I have also reviewed in my book), was not very interested in casting the Austrian Oak for this movie. He wanted Richard Dreyfuss, but Patrick Swayze was also considered, with Bruce Beresford (*Driving Miss Daisy*) as director. Even David Cronenberg was later approached to direct and he wanted William Hurt in the leading role.

Cronenberg made an interesting comment about his work: "I worked on it for a year and did about 12 drafts. Eventually, we got to a point where Ron Shusett said, 'You know what you've done? You've done the Philip K. Dick version.' I said, 'Isn't that what we're supposed to be doing?' He said, 'No, no, we want to do Raiders of the Lost Ark Go to Mars.'"[45]

When the adaptation of Frank Herbert's SF classic *Dune* (1984), directed by David Lynch, flopped at the box office, De Laurentiis lost his enthusiasm for *Total Recall*. Now, Arnold Schwarzenegger stepped it. He convinced the production company Carolco to buy the rights to the film for $3 million and negotiated a salary of $10–11 million (plus 15% of the profits) to play the leading role, with an unusually high degree of control over the production.

The first thing Schwarzenegger did was to recruit Paul Verhoeven as the director because he was highly impressed by *RoboCop*, now a classic SF action movie and one of the most sophisticated movies in the action genre ever made. Verhoeven brought in Gary Goldman to develop the final draft of the screenplay and hired many of his collaborators on *RoboCop*, including actor Ronny Cox, cinematographer Jost Vacano, production designer William Sandel and special effects designer Rob Bottin.

With Verhoeven on board, the film became highly violent, rude and shockingly brutal. Verhoeven likes to shock his audience and the final script of *Total Recall* gave the energetic director several ways to do it. There are so many scenes with death and violence in this movie that Verhoeven again had trouble getting a rating below X. Furthermore, this movie is one of the last major Hollywood blockbusters to make large-scale use of miniature effects rather than computer-generated imagery. And, of course, Verhoeven was again attacked by feminist critics, especially because of one scene between Schwarzenegger and his wife Sharon Stone and the sarcastic comment "Consider this as a divorce" after he shot her in the head.

Even after 28 years, there are still plenty of articles discussing whether the movie is all a dream or reality for Quaid. The white light at the end is taken as an example of the dream theory – Quaid will be lobotomised – and Goldsmith's last track called *End of a Dream* can be also be taken as a hint. But the name of the track can also be the result of a dialogue between Quaid and Melina after the showdown. Quaid asks her "What if this all is a dream?" and she wanted to kiss before they wake up.

Viewers can decide what they want to believe and look for proof of their own theories in the movie. There are enough details for both theories and it is another sign of Verhoeven's genius that he created this ambiguous ending.

*Total Recall* is indeed a very rude and brutal movie, and it is not as good as *RoboCop*, but it is still one of the greatest SF action movies ever. Schwarzenegger is playing one of his best roles, there are so many astonishing action scenes in it (I am big fan of the "cat-fight" between Rachel Ticotin and Sharon Stone), the visual effects are still mind-blowing, and the idea that this all might be a dream is very clever. Last but not least, Jerry Goldsmith's music is one of the best aspects of this movie.

## The music

Jerry Goldsmith said about this score in an interview: *"Total Recall* was some of the best music I've written for a film. I was impressed with myself, even though I rarely listen to what I've finished. I'd written enough notes in that score for a Bruckner symphony! After that, I wanted a change from all of the action films I'd been doing. I realized that I wanted to do "people" pictures again, and held out until I got *The Russia House, Sleeping with the Enemy,* and *Love Field,* movies where I could get lyrical again. *The Russia House* is now my favourite score, while my work for *Medicine Man* has some very lyrical moments."[46]

To save money, the producers sent Jerry Goldsmith to Germany to record the music with a Munich orchestra. Goldsmith was not very happy with the performance; the orchestra was not familiar with his complex style of composing and orchestrating. Therefore, the recording was brought to end and Goldsmith went back to London to record the score with the National Philharmonic Orchestra which was more used to Goldsmith's style. YouTube features the track *Clever Girl* performed by the Munich Orchestra, so this version can be compared with the later version on the CD.

Goldsmith also admitted that the powerful main theme was a reminder of the *Conan* motif. The score consists of a lot of action pieces, and there is even more music on the Deluxe Edition that lasts nearly 74 minutes. The best action tracks are *Clever Girl, The Big Jump* and *The Hologram* (I especially like the electronics here which sound like a metronome clicking).

What makes this score unique is the balance between the straightforward action-packed tracks and the more lyrical tracks such as *A New Life.* One of the best of these lyrical tracks is *The Mutant* when rebel leader Kuato psychically invades Quaid's mind and reveals the true function of the machine buried beneath the mountain that will finally bring air to the Mars. This track is a perfect example of visual storytelling in music!

In some tracks, Goldsmith uses a composing technique to transform the punches into music; not a new idea, but highly effective when watching these scenes with the music. Because of the high amount of chase scenes, the score is massively action driven with a dominance of the brass and the percussion sections. What makes this score very special is again Jerry Goldsmith's ability to combine the sound of the traditional symphonic orchestra with modern electronics.

*Total Recall* was the start of a very inspiring collaboration between Paul Verhoeven and Jerry Goldsmith and it is so sad that these two highly creative people did not work on more projects together. Jerry Goldsmith died and Paul Verhoeven seems no longer to be as welcome in politically correct Hollywood these days. However, I am sure that Hollywood could use a director like him now because of his sense of visuals and drama and his ability to create very action-packed movies.

I have recently felt bored when watching action movies. It is all about the latest special effects, but real storytelling is not often happening these days. Exceptions to this are *Ant-Man"* (2015, which I greatly enjoyed), *Wonder Woman* (2017, because of the actress Gal Gadot and its humour), and Christopher Nolan's non-Batman movies.

The best action track of the score is the penultimate one *End of a Dream.* This track, now 28 years old, is still one of the best action tracks ever written. Goldsmith drives the orchestra through a tour de force that is astonishing because of the musical complexity of this piece and the intense feeling it gives you when listening to this track while watching the movie or apart from the movie on the CD. With *Total Recall* Jerry Goldsmith raised the bar for other composers of action scores, but for himself as well.

## 33. JAWS – WHEN A THEME MADE THE AUDIENCE LAUGH

In my opinion, John Williams composed his best scores in the 1970s. With *Jaws*, the composer created a theme that people recognise as soon as the orchestra starts playing and mostly start to laugh because the theme is so famous and everybody knows what is coming. There is a clip on YouTube with John Williams conducting the Boston Pops, and someone commented: "You know you've made an awesome theme song when only the first note is played, and people instantly figured out what it is."

I was attending a concert of John Williams's music played at the Royal Albert Hall, and when the *Jaws* motif was played the audience started to laugh because they know the theme so well. It was funny to observe: a theme for a man-eating shark making people laugh, but I assume they recognised the famous theme and the fun the conductor had with it, and it was so entertaining.

## The movie

There is a joke in the movie world that with *Psycho* Alfred Hitchcock took away the joy of taking a shower, and with *Jaws* Spielberg took away the joy of swimming. *Jaws* is based on a novel by Peter Benchley. The book tells the story of a large white shark that attacks a small resort town. Three men ultimately try to kill the fish, so it is mostly a man against nature story.

The book is based on Benchley's interest in shark attacks after he learned about the exploits of shark fisherman Frank Mundus in 1964. When I was reading the book a few years ago, I was surprised that Benchley wrote parts of the story from the shark's perspective, so you can read how the fish feels when it is swimming alone through the water: an unusual perspective. A main part of the plot is also Sheriff Brody's marital problems , which was skipped in the screenplay.

Richard D. Zanuck and David Brown, producers at Universal Pictures, heard about the novel and became interested in it. The producers purchased the movie rights in 1973, before the book's publication, for approximately $175,000. Initially veteran director John Sturges was considered, but the young director Steven Spielberg very much wanted the job. Spielberg had just directed his first feature, *The Sugarland Express* (1974), which some people still think is Spielberg's best movie. Critics also recognise that *Jaws* is similar to Spielberg's 1971 television film *Duel*, based on a script by SF legend Richard Matheson.

Steven Spielberg wanted to stay with the novel's basic plot and focused on the shark hunt. Author Benchley wrote three drafts of the script and then other writers took over. It was Spielberg's suggestion that Brody was afraid of water, a very interesting idea. Spielberg's friend Carl Gottlieb, initially hired to introduce some comedy aspects to the script, became the main writer in the end.

The script for each scene was typically finished the night before it was shot, after Gottlieb had dinner with the director and members of the cast and crew to decide what would go into the film and what would not. Many sections of dialogue originated from the actors' improvisations during these meals, most notably Roy Scheider's line "You're gonna need a bigger boat" when they, and also we as the audience, see the shark for the first time. The whole production was a nightmare at times, as is clear from various articles that have been written. There is no need to discuss the production further, so let's concentrate on the music.

## The music

John Williams's music for *Jaws* has been ranked by the American Film Institute as the sixth greatest score. The main "shark" theme, a simple alternating pattern of two notes – variously identified as E and F or F and F sharp – became a classic piece of suspense music, synonymous with approaching danger.

Williams described the theme as "grinding away at you, just as a shark would do, instinctual, relentless, unstoppable." [47] The piece was performed by tuba player Tommy Johnson. When asked why the melody was written in such a high register and not played by the more appropriate French horn, Williams responded that he wanted it to sound "a little more threatening". When Williams first demonstrated his idea to Spielberg, playing just the two notes on a piano, Spielberg was said to have laughed, thinking that it was a joke, but later the director said that without Williams' score the film would have been only half as successful.

There is also plenty of influence of classical music in the score, mostly for rapid, percussive string playing as in *La Mer* by Claude Debussy, mostly in *Play of the Waves*, or Igor Stravinsky's *The Rite of Spring*. Similar manners of composing by Stravinsky and Williams can be heard, especially in the more atonal passages for the action and suspense tracks.

There are different versions of the score available. I have the MCA album comprising twelve tracks, starting with the *Main Title* and the famous motif, played on the tuba, but also balanced by strings, the piano, the brass section and the flute. This track transforms a surprise shark attack into a real musical masterpiece.

The score has plenty of action tracks, such as the first sudden death in *Chrissie's Death* (track 2). Track 3 *Promenade* is a more classical piece, and the subtitle *Tourists on The Menu* is a good example of Williams's sense of humour. Track 4 *Out to Sea* is a beautiful piece that starts the journey to kill the shark.

Track 5 *The Indianapolis story* is a dark and frightening piece. There is still a controversy over who deserves the credit for the famous Indianapolis dialogue scene. Howard Sackler came up with the story of Quint being a survivor of the World War II USS Indianapolis disaster. Spielberg described the ideas as a collaboration between Sackler, John Milius and actor Robert Shaw, who was also a playwright. According to Spielberg, Milius turned Sackler's speech into a monologue, which was then rewritten by Shaw. Gottlieb gives primary credit to Shaw, downplaying Milius's contribution, but that could also be a result of these two writers' different political views.

In the next track called *Sea Attack Number One*, we have a tremendous five-minute action piece, now 40 years old but still highly enjoyable. When the music opens with the string and the bass (there is even a harp in the background!) after 40 seconds, you see the full size of the shark for the first time on screen, and the music erupts triumphantly.

Track 7 *One Barrel Chase* opens with the *Jaws* motif. The scene shows us Robert Shaw's huge surprise as the shark dives down with more than two barrels attached to him. Spielberg initially wanted first Lee Marvin but he did not accept the role, so the producers recommended Robert Shaw. After seeing the movie, it is hard to imagine any other actor playing Quint.

Casting Hooper with Richard Dreyfuss was George Lucas's idea. Spielberg worked with Dreyfuss again on *Close Encounters* two years later. Roy Scheider became interested in the project when Spielberg talked with a screenwriter at a party about having the shark jump onto a boat, a scene that is one of the weakest in the movie. Spielberg was initially apprehensive about hiring Scheider, fearing he would portray Brody as a tough guy because of his performance in William Friedkin's police thriller *The French Connection* (1971), which made the actor very popular.

Track 8 *Preparing the Cage* shows us the scene in which Hooper gets into a cage to kill the shark. In the book, Hooper dies seeing his blood, but in the movie, he survives. Track 9 *Night Search* is classical suspense music, greatly written by Williams, and with a shocking musical effect towards the very end of the track.

Track 10 *The Underwater Siege* underscores the shark attack on the cage, and the last track *Hand to Hand Combat* shows the final attack. The musical underscoring of the fight between Brody armed with a rifle and the approaching shark armed just with his teeth and still hungry to kill another man is marvellous. The music for the dead shark sinking to the seabed is also close to perfection: Williams uses the piano to underscore the pieces of the shark's body slowly sinking, like snowflakes falling to the ground.

*Jaws* was one of the first blockbusters. The movie was a huge success and advanced the careers of Spielberg and Williams. The sequel had just a few good scenes and a nice score by Williams, but the first *Jaws* score will always be remembered as one of John Williams's best scores.

## 34. Batman – Tim Burton's better adaptation

1989 was a good year: the Berlin Wall came down, Communism finally lost and the world saw Tim Burton's first *Batman* with Michael Keaton as the Dark Knight. Since Christopher Nolan created his very successful *Dark Knight* trilogy, critics and movie fans argue over which Batman actor Michael Keaton or Christian Bale is better and which movies are better. So, let's start again with some comments about the film.

### The movie

It is hard to compare these two directors and movies. Tim Burton's first *Batman* movie is more an action movie and the first serious adaptation of *Batman*. Michael Keaton is a fabulous actor and right for this role. He could convince the audience that Batman is not just a Dark Knight, but also a successful businessman with his manners and professional way of dealing with people.

Christopher Nolan is one of the best directors around today. His approach to creating a serious *Batman* movie again after the over-the-top movies by Joel Schumacher (*Batman Forever*, 1995 and *Batman & Robin*, 1997) focused heavily on the dark side of the Batman universe. Perhaps to avoid anything that might point in the direction of Joel Schumacher's *Batman* movies, Nolan avoided all humour.

Sometimes you get the feeling that his Dark Night is a character from Shakespeare, and I think the ending of *Dark Knight* is not convincing: Batman persuades Gordon to preserve Harvey Dent's heroic image by holding Batman responsible for the killing. That is a not compelling idea. I think that Christopher Nolan's non-Batman movies such as *Inception* (2010) and *Interstellar* (2014) are far better.

So, back to 1989: Jack Nicholson gives a marvellous performance as The Joker, but compared to Heath Ledger, Nicholson's Joker is more of a comic character. Ledger's character is a dangerous one because here Nolan shows us how one single bad guy with absolutely no morals could destroy an entire society. Nicholson's Joker is a gangster, Ledger's Joker is a terrorist and portrayed as a virus that, even though destroyed, might have infected people so that they follow his ideas.

## The music

Tim Burton's favourite composer was again hired to compose the music. Danny Elfman's score is not very sophisticated in the sense of having a lot of melodies or artificially composed action tracks; it is simple and sometimes very loud, but in its approach very effective. The whole score is dominated by one simplistic theme – a four-note minor key ascent and two-note major key descent – the so-called Batman march.

The original soundtrack album I have consists of 21 tracks. In 2010 La-La Land Records released a complete album with two CDs. For me, Elfman's *Batman* score is one of his best scores. The one he wrote for the sequel *Batman Returns* (1992) is slightly better because a choir is used in it and the plot gives Elfman more scenes to compose melodramatic music for. Burton directed the sequel like an opera, and the music follows suit, especially in the grand finale.

The first *Batman* score has more straightforward action tracks such as *Roof Fight, First Confrontation, Clown Attack, Batman to The Rescue, Attack Of The Batwing* (listen to the clangs at the end) and the last action track called *The Final Confrontation.*

Elfman used a fine combination of strings with a lot of brass and percussion and in the end a sampled organ to create a gothic atmosphere, which can also be heard in *Up The Cathedral* and *Descent Into Mystery*, one of the score's highlights. Elfman, his orchestrator Steve Bartek and conductor Shirley Walker are good at using the choir in this scene.

Even though *Batman* is very much an action-driven score, there are a few lyrical tracks such as *Flowers, The Joker's Poem* and *Love Theme* (this track includes *Scandalous* by Prince). A fabulous track that shows a wicked sense of humour is *Waltz to the Death* for a wonderful scene in which Batman is fighting against another of the Joker's killers, and in parallel Joker Jack is dancing with Kim Basinger. You can hear this waltz, the motif for the Joker, first in *Kitchen, Surgery, Face-Off* when Joker Jack kills his boss Jack Palance.

With *Batman* Elfman was becoming a high-class composer, and this score

# 35. Great Expectations – How a girl wants to get picked up

I decided to put another Patrick Doyle soundtrack into my book after discussing a lot of action scores. *Great Expectations* is perhaps the composer's most unusual score. The movie is still popular because of a very romantic kissing in the rain scene and Doyle's music for it. This *Kissing in the Rain* is the track I mostly listen to from this score.

## The movie

*Great Expectations* (1988) is a contemporary film adaptation of Charles Dickens's novel, co-written and directed by Alfonso Cuarón and starring Ethan Hawke, Gwyneth Paltrow and Robert De Niro.

Dickens's novel takes place in London between 1812 and 1827, but the screenwriter Mitch Glazer switched the plot from 19th-century London to 1990s New York and changed the name of the male character from Pip to Finn. The character of Miss Havisham was also renamed Nora Dinsmoor. The voice-overs were not in the original screenplay, but once the film was edited producer Art Linson (who in 1987 gave us Brian De Palma's *The Untouchables*) felt these were needed. David Mamet, screenwriter of *The Untouchables*, wrote the voice-overs but was not credited in the final film.

I am not a big fan of voice-overs in general. I think they are mostly used because the writer or director is not able to create a scene that speaks for itself. David & Jerry Zucker and Jim Abrahams made great fun of the typically serious voice-overs in classic film noir movies in their famous *Naked Police* series and the *Naked Gun* trilogy with Leslie Nielson.

Charles Dickens is one of the most famous English authors. *Oliver Twist* is widely read in schools, but I think that the time of Dickens and his books are over so I normally try to avoid reading Dickens novels or watching adaptations of his books.

Placing the plot of *Great Expectation* in the 1990s was a great idea, and Cuarón is such a talented director that I enjoyed this movie and was immediately caught up in it. Cuarón is also the director of the third *Harry* was the first step towards becoming an iconic figure in the film music industry. With *Beetlejuice* (1988) and four years earlier *Pee-wee's Big Adventure*, both directed by Tim Burton, Elfman showed that his effective and often unusual orchestrated music underscored Burton's weird stories perfectly. With *Batman*, Elfman made a huge leap forward and this soundtrack is still very popular today.

For me, Danny Elfman's music to *Batman* is better than Hans Zimmer's contribution to the series: it is more dynamic, has a better theme, is astonishing in the use of various percussions and has a better sense of humour.

Potter movie (*Harry Potter and the Prisoner of Azkaban*, 2004), in my opinion the best of the franchise, and also directed the SF movie *Gravity* (2013) starring George Clooney and Sandra Bullock.

I do not want to talk too much about the plot and the movie; people should watch it and enjoy its twists. The kissing in the rain scene is very popular, a highly erotic and wonderfully directed scene. I remember a female friend of mine saying to me after talking about this scene: "That is the way every girl wants to get picked up!"

## The music

Buying the soundtrack is a little confusing because there are two albums, one "soundtrack" with mostly songs written for the movie, and the "score" with Patrick Doyle's music. It took me considerable effort to finally get the score and this CD is now sold out.

The CD consists of 22 tracks and is perhaps the Doyle score that shows the most variety. Imagine that the composer was diagnosed with leukaemia shortly after finishing this work, maybe the reason why the score consists mostly of sad and melancholic music.

Doyle hired guitarist John Williams to play some tracks, and this works very well. Because people get confused about the name, let me give some background information about John Williams: born in 1941 in Melbourne, Australia to an English father, Len Williams, who later founded the London Guitar School, and Malaan (née Ah Ket), a daughter of Melbourne barrister William Ah Ket, the Williams family moved 1952 to England. Williams was initially taught guitar by his father who was an accomplished guitarist, and later attended the Royal College of Music in London from 1956 to 1959, studying piano because the college did not have a guitar department at the time.

If you look at Williams's discography, it is surprising how often he has contributed to soundtracks, but *Great Expectations* is still one of his most popular works. The tracks Williams played on are track 4 *Estella's Theme* (the main theme), track 5 *Ain't Love Grand*, track 6 *A Walk in The Park*, track 13 *A Toast*, track 14 *Benefactor*, and track 17 *It Was Just My Memory Of It*.

Doyle also used the electronic wind Instrument played by Phil Todd on some tracks and used the piano in track 9 *Joe Leaves*, a track just for the piano. One of the highlights of the score is the aria called *I Saw No Shadow of Another Parting*. This track gives the impression that Doyle should one day compose an opera. This track is quite impressive, performed by famous New Zeeland opera singer Kiri Te Kanawa.

American singer-songwriter Tori Amos composed the song *Siren*. She also contributed to the score album with the first track called *Finn*, which sets the tone of the movie with its whispering voice and on track 3 called *Paradiso Perduto*.

One of the most delightful performances of the main theme is track 11 *Pyramid of Pain*. Here the main theme is played by the orchestra without guitar or vocals, a pretty nice track. Track 15 *Lustig Dies* underscores the last scene for Robert De Niro, a piece that will touch you. This is one of the few times that the score erupts out of its mostly quiet style.

The most famous track is track 8 *Kissing in the Rain*, with vocals by Miriam Stockley. The South African-born British singer and composer has contributed to several film soundtracks, including *The Lord of the Rings: The Fellowship of the Ring* (2001), the Mike Figgis drama *One Night Stand* (1997, with a wonderful performance by action star Wesley Snipes and German actor and Klaus Kinski's daughter Nastassja Kinski as a couple in love for one night) and the British miniseries *The 10th Kingdom* (2000).

The dramaturgical structure of *Kissing in the rain* is admirable. The music stops when Finn enters the restaurant and then starts again when they dance. When the loving couple go out into the rain, the music erupts with Miriam Stockley's voice, before it slows down again when the couple in bed. What a wonderful scene, what a wonderful track! This is one of the best tracks Doyle ever composed, and I never get tired of listening to it. The song was sampled in the song *RoboCop* on Kanye West's 2008 album *808s & Heartbreak*.

*Great Expectations* is one of the few excellent romantic movies. Ethan Hawke and Gwyneth Paltrow are very good together, and even though the movie was not a box office hit, it is clear what a good director can bring out of a novel that is over 100 years old. Gwyneth Paltrow gives one of her best performances in this movie.

One of the reasons that this movie is still so popular is Patrick Doyle's music, especially his kissing in the rain music and that scene. It really shows what the magic of love is all about!

## 36. First Blood – Birth of Sylvester Stallone's
### Second Legend

When you look back over Jerry Goldsmith's career, there is no doubt that 1982 was the best year of his career. He composed five scores that year: *Poltergeist*, *The Secret of NIMH*, *The Challenge*, *Inchon* and *First Blood*. If you look at the scores included in my book, three of these are presented.

**The movie**

While writing this book, I was reading the Kirk Douglas autobiography called *The Ragman's Son*, which I really recommend if you have not yet read it. It is a great book written in a unique style full of romance, sadness, tragedy and anecdotes. I very much admire Kirk Douglas for hiring Dalton Trumbo as the writer for *Spartacus* even though he had been blacklisted as a Communist sympathiser. When Stanley Kubrick had no scruples taking credit for writing the script, Douglas announced that Trumbo was the writer of the screenplay and helped end the power of the blacklist.

Douglas was considered for the role of Colonel Trautman, but he said that he wanted changes to the script. Stallone, not director Ted Kotcheff, made the final creative decision, as Douglas pointed out in his book, and rejects Douglas's idea of Trautman killing Rambo. Douglas's idea was that the Colonel realised what kind of Frankenstein-like creature he had created and wanted to end his life.

Even though I admire Douglas as an actor and for his body of work, I think this idea shows that he did not get the idea of the script. Compared to the sequel, Rambo is not a killing machine. He is an innocent character and just started going crazy because he was being tortured by the local police.

In my opinion, the most important scene is when Sheriff Teasle, played by Brian Dennehy, tells Rambo that he is not welcomed in the city and has to go. Rambo refuses, so Teasle picks him up, discovers his knife and wants to lock him up. The policemen begin to abuse Rambo. When they want to cut his hair and Rambo sees the knife, he has memories of torture in Vietnam and freaks out. This scene is underscored by one of the most excellent tracks in the score called *The Razor*.

Even after he escapes, the abuse continues and Rambo is hunted like an animal without having done anything. In my opinion, he is just acting in self-defence but is slowly losing his mind and overacts due to his will to survive. Trautman, played by Richard Crenna, finally stops him as he is about to kill the sheriff. So why should Trautman kill him?

The movie criticises how American war veterans are treated. Rambo explains that they were blaming him for doing his job and not blaming the politicians who started the war. So if Trautman had let Rambo have his meal, he would have left the city and nobody would have been killed. Another aspect to consider is that the movie is also focusing on the hostile attitude of more right-wing people towards "hippie"-looking people because Rambo was also attacked for his long hair. The same motifs are shown at the end of *Easy Rider* (1969).

Years ago, I read the 1972 novel by David Morrell[48]. Canadian-born writer Morrell worked as an English professor at the University of Iowa in 1970 before he gave up his job and concentrated on writing. The book was inspired by hearing about the experiences of his students who had fought in Vietnam. The character's name was developed from the Rambo apple Morrell's wife brought home while Morrell was struggling to find a suitable name for the main character.

In the DVD commentary, Morell comments that one of the inspirations for Rambo was Second World War hero Audie Murphy. In the end, Rambo gets wounded in the shooting with Teasle and both die. Trautman tells Teasle that he killed Rambo and the sheriff feels a moment of affection for the man he had killed.

While I was reading it, I thought that it was not a suitable ending for a movie because it is too intellectual, especially in the way Rambo wants to kill himself in the book. You can decide for yourself which ending is more convincing – the movie or the book – when you read the novel.

### The music

If you listen to the main theme, I think the idea of Rambo as an innocent character might be right. It is one of Jerry Goldsmith's most lyrical main themes and the track *Home Coming* is a beautiful example of transforming the feeling of loneliness and peacefulness into music. The guitar is exactly the right instrument for this approach, while the trumpet reminds you of the military aspects of the plot.

For this score, there are also different CDs to buy. I recommend buying the two-CD set by Intrada, which has 19 tracks including the song *It's a long road* performed by Canadian singer Dan Hill with lyrics by South African songwriter Hal Shaper, an instrumental version of *It's a long road* and the theme from *First Blood* (a pop version). In the liner notes to this CD, Douglass Fake gave a very personal insight into the history of Intrada, a very interesting read, about how it took 25 years to present a complete release of *First Blood Finally*. Fake explained how Jerry Goldsmith "cut significant bars off the ends of certain cues to allow for smooth edits into other unrelated cues, removed the opening bars of other cues for similar reasons and completely re-organized the sequence apart from the picture." [49]

Compared to the sequel in particular, this score has the right balance between the more lyrical tracks and the now famous action tracks such as *Hanging On* (perhaps the best track), *Over the Cliff* (a great piece), *Escape Route* and *The Truck*. The already mentioned *The Razor* is one of most interestingly orchestrated tracks. It slowly builds up the suspense, transforms Rambo's terrifying memories of torture in Vietnam in atonal music, then mostly underscores the violent action with percussion and just rhythm. When Rambo escapes with the motorbike, you can hear the powerful first blood theme in a full orchestral arrangement.

Owing to the dramaturgical structure of the movie, there is plenty of suspense music for the hunting scenes, such as *Mountain Hunt*. Goldsmith uses the piano or the synthetic keyboard to create suspense and transform Rambo's escape on foot into music.

If you compare this first score with the later ones, it is surprising how little Goldsmith in the end uses the main theme. Except for *Mountain Hunt, First Blood* is the longest track, working like a summary of the score and bringing a typical action track in the Goldsmith style with a heavy focus on the percussion.

The action music is Goldsmith at his best, and it is clear how artificially the composer likes to compose his action music. He mostly uses 5/8 and 7/8 time signatures, and the tracks are highly enjoyable. One of my favourite pieces is the shorter track *The Truck*.

Unlike the score of the sequel, this score does not feature heavy electronics. The music to the second part is highly action-orientated (*The Jump* from *First Blood II* is one of Goldsmith's best action tracks), and the third score is a good mixture of action and more lyrical pieces with beautiful end credits music that was not used in the film.

Jerry Goldsmith died on 21 July 2004 after a long battle with cancer. Brian Tyler took over and composed the music for the fourth instalment, an unnecessarily violent movie with gore and splatter scenes to compete with sadistic horror movies such as *Hostel* (2005).

Even though Stallone directed this movie and tried to bring the franchise to a good ending (Rambo is going home), the violence in the showdown is so over the top that this sequel can be considered the worst of the whole series.

One final aspect about Kirk Douglas: the actor considers his western *Lonely are the Brave* (1962), also with a script by Dalton Trumbo, his favourite movie. The movie tells the story of a cowboy who cannot fit into the modern society and refuses to be part of it. He later becomes an outlaw and is hunted down by a local sheriff, played by Walter Matthau.

*Lonely are the Brave* starts with the idea that the main character wants to visit a friend and then the trouble starts. There are a lot of similarities with *First Blood*. In the end, the cowboy's horse is severely injured and the sheriff kills it. The wounded cowboy is taken to hospital. It is unclear whether he will survive his injuries.

Jerry Goldsmith composed the music to this western too, and his score was greatly praised by critics and colleagues alike. Bernard Herrmann said that the music was too good for the movie. In this western, the main character was also hunted by helicopter, like Rambo in *First Blood*. If you compare both soundtracks, there are a great many similarities between the two scores.

So, perhaps Douglas developed the idea that Rambo should get killed because his cowboy in *Lonely are the Brave* might not have survived the movie either?

# 37. La La Land – And here's to the fools who dream

I was thinking a great deal about whether I should include *La La Land* (2016) because it is not the kind of classic instrumental soundtrack I mostly wanted to discuss in this book. This is therefore the only review of a musical, but because *La La Land* is one of the most enjoyable movies in recent years, I decided to include a review of this score as an example of how to create a wonderfully entertaining film that also has an ending that makes you think.

## The movie

I had heard a lot about *La La Land* before finally seeing it. In general, I am not a big fan of watching musicals on screen, I prefer to see them on stage, but I was curious to see it because so many people were talking about it. I had not read any reviews of it beforehand, I had never watched a movie by this director, listened to any music by its composer and could not even remember if I had ever watched a movie with Emma Stone in it.

Of course, I had seen a few movies starring Ryan Gosling, for example *The Ides of March* (2011) with George Clooney, which I did not like very much, but I loved *The Notebook* (2004), not because of Gosling, more because of Rachel McAdams, and I remain a big fan of hers. So, I went to see *La La Land* with no expectations and out of sheer curiosity.

It is usually always a little awkward when you see a movie and then suddenly the actors start singing because there is generally no reason for doing so. *La La Land* is also different in this aspect. The start with the traffic jam in the always annoying traffic in Los Angeles, the people getting tired and bored and then finally starting to sing because they just want to entertain themselves, first slowly, then with more and more passion, and finally more people (including a combo playing in a van) joining in… was such a great idea and a great beginning!

While watching this scene and the singers' passion in performing it, I immediately began to like the movie. I was also captivated by the score: this is precisely the kind of music I want to hear in a musical, slightly-jazzy, dynamic and fun to listen to, just pure entertainment.

The title *La La Land* refers to the city of Los Angeles, but is also an idiom for being out of touch with reality. This is only the second movie directed by Damien Chazelle, born in 1985, after *Whiplash* (2014, also about jazz). He wrote the script in 2010 but was unable to find a studio willing to finance production. Following the success with *Whiplash*, Chazelle was finally able to do it. Justin Hurwitz, also the composer on *Whiplash*, met Chazelle at Harvard. They were playing in the same band and then became roommates.

In an interview, Chazelle explained the idea behind the movie: "I think now more than ever we need hope and romance on the screen, and I think there's something about musicals that get at something that only movies can do. That idea of movies as a dreamland, movies as the language of our dreams and movies as a way of expressing a world in which you break into song, that emotions can violate the rules of reality. There is something very poetic about Los Angeles I think, about a city that is built by people with these unrealistic dreams and people who kind of just put it all on the line for that."[50]

Chazelle admitted that it was a challenge to produce a musical in today's world, but he was able to fall back on the timelessness of classic musicals to find his way. "*La La Land* should also be a homage to all the creative people who moved to Los Angeles to chase their dreams" [51], said the director, and because of that, the film also contains numerous visual allusions to Hollywood classics such as *Broadway Melody of 1940* (1940), *Singin' in the Rain* (1952, with Gene Kelly's classic song scene) and *The Band Wagon* (1953).

The music is not only the reason why *La La Land* has been so successful. The screenplay is very well written and the cast fits perfectly. The story has a good sense of humour, but also a fair amount of sad moments. Emma Stone is astonishing in her role. For me, the best part is the ending, especially the last minutes of the movie in the *Epilogue* scene. After seeing it, I watched it again two weeks later. I cannot remember ever having done that before, and these closing minutes touched me even more the second time. Well done! This is great storytelling!

## The music

The score was composed and orchestrated by Justin Hurwitz. The soundtrack has 15 tracks and starts with *Another Day of Sun*, the energetic dance number from the opening scene and the only cast song. This first track sets the tone for the rest of the score with the lyrics emphasising the importance of dreaming. This feel-good song is a perfect start for the album and the movie.

The next track *Someone in the crowd* is the second highlight. Music should tell a story, and this song is exactly doing it: "Somewhere there's a place / Where I find who I'm gonna be / Somewhere that's just waiting to be found", perhaps summarise the idea of life as a journey. Emma Stone and her roommates give a lively and amusing performance in the scene. What a great scene!

Track 3 *Mia & Sebastian's Theme* is a wonderful piano track. This theme is a well-balanced piece with a melody that you will never forget after you hear it. Track 4 *A Lovely Night* is the next highlight. The music underscores the first real scene between Mia and Sebastian and captures perfectly the playfulness of their dealings with one other up to then. When the music suddenly breaks out into a tap-dancing number, we have one of the best scenes in the movie.

There are two versions of *City of Stars*: track 6 with Ryan Gosling alone and track 9 with Ryan and Emma Stone. This song won the Academy Award for Best Song, and deservedly so. Track 12 *Audition (The Fools Who Dream)* is the last song on the album and the best song of the score. When Emma Stone is asked at an audition to tell a story, it becomes the story of her dreams and disillusions. This scene is the first step to her ultimate success and a magical scene in the movie!

There are a lot of instrument tracks on this score. I have already mentioned track 3, but my personal favourites are *Planetarium* (track 7) and in particular track 13 *Epilogue* (with some vocals at the end).

When I was watching the *Epilogue* scene, an idea came to mind: German opera composer Richard Wagner created what is known as the Tristan chord for his opera *Tristan und Isolde*. A chord normally consists of three notes, and they all have to be played, but because Tristan and Isolde are constantly interrupted when they are together, Wagner did not let all three notes in this chord be played during the opera until the final scene. In just the last scene, the death scene, Wagner lets the orchestra play the full chord. The music expresses the idea that the couple is finally together, together at the moment of death.

When you now listen to the last scene of *La La Land* and watch how Sebastian plays his melody, I got the impression that he did not play the last note. He did not finish the theme in this scene because he and Mia did not come together in the end.... Might this be true? I look forward to receiving comments about this.

For me, *La La Land* is not only a great feel-good movie, but it also tells a wonderful story about two creative people who believe in their dreams. Like each good movie, *La La Land* also has its sad moments, and the last scene is one of the saddest moments I have seen in the cinema recently. They smile at one other, but you can see they think that they have just – excuse me – fucked up their chance of being happy together. Is Mia really happy after this scene and can she continue with her life as nothing happened? I doubt it; her smile is not a real smile. It is the smile you put on your face when you are trying to hide your tears.

# 38. VERTIGO – ALFRED HITCHCOCK'S BEST MOVIE

You can argue about which of *Psycho, North by Northwest* or *Vertigo* is the best Bernard Herrmann score for a Hitchcock movie and you can, of course, argue about which is Alfred Hitchcock's best movie. I have made my choice: *Vertigo* is Hitchcock's best movie and Bernard Herrmann's ultimate masterpiece, which is why I have chosen a picture of a live performance of *Vertigo* at the Southbank Centre in London on 25 June 2017 as the cover for my book.

## The movie

For many years, *Psycho* was my favourite Hitchcock movie because it is astonishing what Hitchcock did with Robert Bloch's novel. *Psycho* is not only one of the best Hitchcock crime thrillers, but it is the ultimate thriller and established a whole new genre known as slasher movies. Without *Psycho*, there would be no *Halloween*.

What makes *Vertigo* unique is not only Bernard Herrmann's haunting and melodramatic music, but the whole composition of this movie and the tragic ending in particular. Perhaps this ending was one of the reasons why the movie was not a huge box office success, but to be honest this unhappy ending gave the movie just the right kick and another reason why *Vertigo* is Hitchcock's ultimate masterpiece.

I read the novel by the French writers Pierre Boileau and Thomas Narcejac a few years ago and was really disappointed by it. The book is good, but not a masterpiece. Without the movie, this novel would be long forgotten. You can understand the genius of Hitchcock in the way he changed just one aspect of the storytelling (the letter scene), which has a considerable effect. I think there are still some among the younger generation who have perhaps not yet seen *Vertigo*, so I will not say too much about it. In Wikipedia, you can read about the editing of this scene and will discover that a good movie is sometimes a result of luck and the decisions taken by people other than the director.

Hitchcock blamed James Stewart for the film's failure because the actor, then aged 50, might have looked too old to play a convincing love interest for Kim

Novak, who at 25 was half of his age. But perhaps it was also part of the role Jimmy Stewart has to play in *Vertigo*: in his fourth and last collaboration with Hitchcock, Stewart – generally cast as the typical American middle-class man – portrays an emotionally weak and obsessed guy who acts in a very dubious way. Maybe this role was too much for the audience at that time, and perhaps this role went too much against the viewing habits of the James Stewart audience and fans back then?

Even Orson Welles did not like the movie very much, preferring *Rear Window* (1954), which shows that even someone like Orson Welles was not able to understand the beauty and perfection of *Vertigo*.

The movie was shot in San Francisco, where I lived from 2013 to 2015, and *Vertigo* sightseeing tours can be taken in the city. It is still possible to explore the unique atmosphere of San Francisco, even though being a tech hub has made it nearly impossible for hipsters and artists to be able to afford to live in the city anymore. A taxi driver born in San Francisco told me that it is losing its special vibe because the new people coming in do no longer appreciate the city's history and its qualities.

**The music**

There are various soundtrack editions with the score. I prefer Herrmann as the conductor of his music because he has the best understanding of the perfect interpretation and tempi of the score. For example, if you listen to the soundtrack of *North by Northwest* conducted by Laurie Johnson and compare it with Herrmann's conducting, it is clear that Johnson's style is far too slow.

Recently a nearly complete *Vertigo* CD has come out conducted by Joel McNeely, an excellent recording with the right tempi, but I still prefer Herrmann's recording even though McNeely's has more tracks than the original one. The original score for the movie has 42 cues, which comprise about 74 minutes of the music heard in the film.

The score has a lot of highlights, and each track is worth listening to, but I would like to recommend a few here. The first *Vertigo* CD I bought contained 11 tracks, and I will mostly focus on this release, but there is also an expanded release with 16 tracks, both of which are conducted by Muir Mathieson. Scottish-born Mathieson was hired to conduct *Vertigo* after a musicians' strike in Los Angeles made it impossible to record the score there, but the score could not be completed in London because the local musicians decided to strike too, therefore the team was forced to move to Vienna. Some critics say that this conductor did not do a good job, for example that there is too much romance and not enough energy in his way of conducting. Therefore, an exploration of *Vertigo* starts with finding a proper release of the music.

*Prelude and Rooftop* is also one of the best tracks. The prelude sequence was designed by graphic designer Saul Bass who used spiral motifs in both the title sequence and the movie poster to illustrate the sense of vertigo. The title sequence begins with a section of a woman's face, a close-up of her mouth and then her eyes, looking straight to camera. The right eye is isolated in a close-up, the colour changes to red, the title *Vertigo* comes out of the pupil followed by a spiralling figure afterwards, before the still blinking eye, so that it looks more real, vanishes.

This is an amazing introductory scene combined with Herrmann's music. If you have ever seen the sequel to Michael Crichton's SF *Westworld* (1973) called *Futureworld* (1976), it is evident that the title sequence is similar to the Hitchcock classic.

Herrmann uses the strings in a fantastic and haunting way, constantly interrupted by the brass section and various percussion instruments. Every time, I am surprised at how he is able to make the musical link between the prelude scene and the immediate rooftop chase because there is no gap between the two tracks. Herrmann now underscores the chase scene, and the audience can experience Scotty's acrophobia for the first time, underscored by Herrmann with a dissonant chord.

*Scotty tails Madeleine* introduces the beautiful, but also sad love theme. This theme, and especially the music when Scotty follows Madeline in the city, has a dark and haunting expression. Hitchcock shot these scenes almost as a silent movie, with minimal dialogue, with just the music driving the emotions here. *Carlotta's Portrait* is a great track for learning how Herrmann is able to build suspense. *The Bay* underscores a crucial scene in the movie, so no comment about this piece or the following tracks. These are very atmospheric pieces, and you have to give too much of the plot away to analyse them.

A few words about *The Nightmare And Dawn* because it is a wonderfully haunting piece, especially when you think about the scene. Are there some similarities to Goldsmith's *Nightmare* music from *The 'Burbs*? You have to decide for yourself. I love the dramaturgical structure of this piece, especially the use of the castanets which are highly effective at creating the haunting atmosphere in the music. After this music, Scotty faces an emotional breakdown.

The highlight of the score is *Scene D'Amour*. In this scene, Scotty is happy to finally see his dream come true. Hitchcock created a perfect scene, wonderfully photographed by Robert Burks. The music perfectly underscores the emotions of the scene.

Hermann created his own *Tristan and Isolde* here: the kiss is the climax, the most intense part of the track, with a beautiful interpretation of the love theme, romantic but also haunting, energetic, nervous, and then finally again very passionate. Overall, you can sense and begin to understand that these happy feelings will not last forever.

*The Necklace, The Return And Finale* brings the showdown. Herrmann underscores the tragic ending in such an emotional way that after the last note was played, the audience at the live performance I attended were so touched that the applause was more enthusiastic than usual. When you listen to the track on a CD, do not be surprised by the quieter part: it is essential for the final scene...

Bernard Herrmann has a formidable sense of drama, and it is a common fact that without his scores, Hitchcock's movies would not be as convincing and touching. Even though *Psycho*, which I have already discussed, is the more popular of Herrmann's Hitchcock scores, in my opinion *Vertigo* is a much more advanced score and demonstrates just what a genius film music composer can do.

Without the score, *Vertigo* would not be as touching. Just watch *Scene D'Amour* without music and then with the music, and you will understand the genius of Bernard Herrmann. There is a rumour that Hitchcock was not very happy that Herrmann's music had such an influence on the movies: both men were geniuses, but also very different in temperament.

It is not surprising therefore that a conflict between the two men ended the most successful relationship between a composer and a director in movie history. If you look at Hitchcock's movies after the break up with Herrmann, the director was never able to establish another long-term collaboration with a composer. Herrmann was able to advance his career after Hitchcock, and the younger generation of New Hollywood directors such as Brian De Palma and Martin Scorsese were aware of the importance of Herrmann's scores in Hitchcock's movies.

Even though I do not discuss Herrmann's 1976 score for *Obsession* in my book, it might be the best score Herrmann composed after his break up with Hitchcock. Check out this passionate and highly energetic score!

# 39. THE MAGNIFICENT SEVEN – THE ULTIMATE WESTERN SCORE

This second and last review of an Elmer Bernstein soundtrack in my book is also his most famous score. It became so popular that it is considered the genuinely iconic western score. If you think of a western score, you will think of this score, and not because the music was used for Marlboro commercials. It is just a perfect score!

## The movie

American director John Sturges is well known for his excellent westerns such as *Bad Day at Black Rock* (1955), *Gunfight at the OK Corral* (1957) and *Last Train from Gun Hill* (1959). *The Magnificent Seven* (1960) was a remake of Akira Kurosawa's Japanese-language film *Seven Samurai* (1954) and is a classic western movie starring Yul Brynner, Eli Wallach and Steve McQueen, and a supporting cast of Charles Bronson, Robert Vaughn, James Coburn, Brad Dexter and the German Horst Buchholz. They play a group of seven American gunfighters hired to protect a small agricultural village in Mexico from a group of marauding native bandits led by Eli Wallach.

There are plenty of entertaining stories about this movie, for example that Brynner as the biggest star in the cast at that time wanted to be treated best, e.g. he wanted to have the best place to stay on set. I also read that McQueen was annoyed by Brynner's behaviour and teased him during the shoot.

Robert Vaughn wrote a great story about the rivalry between Brynner and McQueen: "Brynner, who'd won an Oscar for *The King And I*, was the biggest star – aloof and distant – and accordingly stayed in a private house. The rest of us made do with a motel. The rivalry between McQueen and Brynner was clear from the start. Steve started knocking on my door around 6.30am, an hour before we were due on set. Our conversations were always along the same lines. 'Man,' he would say in that husky whisper, 'did you see Brynner's gun on the set yesterday?' 'I can't say I noticed it, Steve.' 'You didn't notice it? It has a f*****g pearl handle, for God's sake. He shouldn't have a gun like that. It's too f*****g fancy. Nobody's gonna look at anything else with that goddam gun in the picture.' Of course, what Steve meant was

that nobody would be looking at Steve McQueen. Two days later, there was another early-morning knock on the door. 'Did you see the size of Brynner's horse? It's goddam gigantic.' This time I had noticed. 'Actually, Steve, I've got the biggest horse of the Seven.' McQueen shook his head. 'I don't give a f*** about your horse,' he replied. 'It's Brynner's horse I'm worried about.'"
[52]

## The music

Elmer Bernstein's score to *The Magnificent Seven* soon became a classic. The main theme is iconic and was used in commercials for Marlboro cigarettes and in the James Bond movie *Moonraker* as a humorously intended citation. It is interesting that the original soundtrack was not released until it was rerecorded by the composer for the soundtrack of *Return of the Seven* (1966).

In 1994, James Sedares conducted a re-recording of the score performed by The Phoenix Symphony Orchestra. Elmer Bernstein was very pleased with this recording and in the liner notes praised the "tremendous artistry, energy and joy" of this recording that represents almost the complete score. One benefit of this recording is the overture of *The Hallelujah Trail* (1965), a hilarious western parody starring Burt Lancaster and Lee Remick, also directed by John Sturges. For this comedy, Bernstein wrote one of his most entertaining scores with great lyrics by Ernie Sheldon such as "Love a woman, and she loves you / Hallelujah trail / Just do unto her like she wants you to / Hallelujah trail / There ain't no such thing as a perfect man / Hallelujah trail / You girls gotta do the best you can / Hallelujah trail."

Except for the main theme, there is a really beautiful theme for the Mexican villages, heard for the first time in *Council of War* until it gets interrupted by the theme for the banditos, a powerful theme for the bad people around Eli Wallach.

Elmer Bernstein composed lovely music with a lot of Mexican flavour in tracks such as *Toreador* and used a lot of percussion instruments such as bongos, Mexican drums, castanets and marimbas to emphasise the atmosphere of the setting.

An excellent piece is the track *Training* which underscores the gunfighters' training of the Mexicans to handle guns and rifles. Due to the nature of the movie, there are many action tracks. One highlight worth mentioning is *Calvera Killed*. The last track called *Finale* is another variation of the beautiful love theme.

The movie is still great fun to watch even though I do not understand Brynner's last line in the film. In my opinion, it is a little over the top in its approach to introducing tragedy to the whole story. Brynner's costume was so popular that the actor put it on again and played the gunslinger in Michael Crichton's SF thriller *Westworld* (1973) and in the sequel *Futureworld* (1976), that time more of a parody of his role in *Westworld*.

Elmer Bernstein's score became so popular that a lot of western scores nowadays sound just like this one. So, when you hear Bernstein's score for the first time, you will be surprised at how familiar it seems. It was so popular that even Bernstein began to produce sound-alikes for his other western scores. Who can blame him for that? With this soundtrack Bernstein created the definitive western score for American western movies, just as Ennio Morricone did with his scores for the spaghetti western.

It depends what kind of recording you like as to which one to buy – Sedares's recording in excellent quality, or Bernstein's from the 60s with occasionally poor sound quality. Anyway, whatever recording you chose, enjoy this incredible soundtrack from one of the best American film music composers for one of the best American westerns.

# 40. AN AMERICAN TRAIL – JAMES HORNER'S FIRST ANIMATION MOVIE

In putting the soundtracks for this book together, I realised that I had only one score for an animation movie in this book: Jerry Goldsmith's score for *The Secret of NIMH* as my first review. A lot of film music composers have written music for animation movies, and this genre has now a lot of fabulous soundtracks, so I decided to include another animation review. But which one?

I then decided then to write about another James Horner score, especially after attending the fantastic James Horner memorial concert in the Royal Albert Hall in London on 24 October 2017. This concert showed the enthusiastic audience again quite how much Horner and his music are missed.

### The movie

*An American Tail* is a 1986 American animation movie directed by Don Bluth. After Goldsmith's *The Secret of NIMH*, this is the second review of a Don Bluth animation movie review in my book, and both movies have fantastic scores.

I like *The Secret of NIMH* more because of the better plot, the more convincing storytelling and character development, and especially because of its haunting atmosphere. *An American Tail* tells a story for kids, while *The Secret of NIMH* has some scenes that might be a little too scary for children. Feivel Mousekewitz and his Jewish family want to emigrate from the Russian Empire-controlled territory of Ukraine to the United States for freedom and a better life. There is a funny scene explaining the reason in a song called *There Are No Cats In America* (track 3), but anti-Semitism is another reason. Critics mentioned that this was not covered too much in the story. During the journey, Feivel (named after Spielberg's grandfather Fievel) gets lost and has to find a way to re-join them.

*An American Tail* was a box office hit, making it the highest-grossing non-Disney animated film at the time. I have read that this success and the very successful *The Land Before Time* (1988, also with a score by James Horner), and finally Disney's *Who Framed Roger Rabbit* (1988, with a fabulous score by Alan Silvestri), as well as Bluth's departure from their partnership, prompted Spielberg to establish his own animation studio, Amblimation.

The original concept featured an all-animal world, but Bluth wanted something different. He developed the idea that this movie should be more like classic Disney movies such as *The Rescuers* (1977, perhaps better known as the first Bernard and Bianca movie) or *101 Dalmatians* (1961) with an animal world as a society hidden from the humans. Bluth also wanted to go back to the old look of Disney's *Snow White and the Seven Dwarfs* (1937) where the characters were "round, soft and have a cuddly feel". [53]

### The music

In my opinion, James Horner composed his best soundtracks in the 1980s. His style sounded so fresh at times, his melodies were so lovely and lyrical, and his way of using the orchestra was so enjoyable. Spielberg wanted *An American Tail* to be a musical, and Horner was highly excited about doing a score like this: he had just done *Aliens* and now wanted to do something different.

The score was recorded in London by The London Symphony Orchestra and the Choir of King's College. I am personally not a big fan of the songs in *An American Tail*, but compared to other soundtrack composers Horner was so capable at composing songs that the pop version of *Somewhere Out There*, co-composed with Barry Mann with lyrics by Cynthia Weil, and sung by Linda Ronstadt and James Ingram during the end credits, won a Grammy Award, and became one of the most popular songs from an animated feature since the 1950s. How lovely this song still is, was evident at the James Horner concert I mentioned above.

My favourite song in *An American Tail* is *Never Say Never Again*, a lovely melody sung by legendary Canadian actor Christopher Plummer with a heavy accent in this role. What a great piece of music and precisely the way a song for animation movie should be composed.

Feivel's interpretation of *Somewhere Out There*, sung by American child actor Phillip Glasser in a duet with Betsy Cathcart, is just sweet to listen to because neither of the two kids can carry the tune the whole time. That is exactly the reason I love this song much more than the sterile pop version. Track 11 *A Duo* is more of a musical joke because of the way it is sung.

The musical score is James Horner at his best. This movie gave the composer so many scenes to develop beautiful music for that you cannot praise the score enough. Track 1 *Main Title* starts slowly and forms such a lovely atmosphere that you immediately get into it. The influence of classical Russian composers such as Tchaikovsky can be heard, primarily from using the violin in a folk-music style. I am a big fan of the solo violin part at 3'08.

Track 2 *The Cossack Cats* gives us the first action track. Horner's music is fabulous. Track 4 *The Storm* is a four-minute action track that is perfectly developed in its dramaturgical structure and underscores the scene in which Feivel gets thrown overboard and separated from his family. Horner created a haunting atmosphere in this track similar to Goldsmith's *Secret of NIMH*. Track 7 *The Market Place* is lovely because of the use of the main theme in the last 50 seconds of the track. It is interesting that there is not a stand-alone track with the whole main theme; it is spread throughout the score.

The orchestration of track 10 *Releasing the Secret Weapon* reminds me of one of my favourite James Horner scores *The Rocketeer* (1991), but it does not have the elegance of that later score. In the last minute, you can hear the song *There Are No Cats In America* again, but you have to watch the scene to understand it.

The next three tracks called *The Great Fire, Reunited* and *Flying Away and End Credits* are the best tracks in the soundtrack, underscoring the showdown. *Flying Away* is one of my all-time favourite Horner tracks. These three tracks are the highlights of the score.

*Reunited* is a good example of the lyrical melodies Horner was able to compose. These melodies immediately create the atmosphere of a movie and captivate you from the outset. As with the main theme to the ghost movie *Casper* (1995 with Christina Ricci), this is more a kind of a lullaby.

The six-minute track *Flying Away* is the longest and best track. It brings the soundtrack to a beautiful end and is perfectly orchestrated with its lovely themes, its musical structure and the balance of the large orchestra and choir. This is just a fantastic piece of musical storytelling! Imagine that this was Horner's first animation movie and how young he was at the time.

With its six themes *An American Tail* is definitely one of Horner's most structured and most enjoyable scores. If I compare all of Horner's scores for animation movies, I still prefer his music for *Balto* (1995), but there are personal reasons for this. *An American Tail* became a franchise with four movies and video games.

James Horner composed the music for the sequel *Feivel Goes West* (1991), an animated western that I have never watched even though I bought the music. Some critics think that the thematic material for the sequel is better developed than the original one. I will not talk about this here so over to you to find out for yourself!

# 41. POLTERGEIST – BEAUTY AND THE BEAST

Jerry Goldsmith's *Poltergeist* (1982) is another famous score by this composer, one of my all-time favourite soundtracks and another example of what film music can achieve if you have as gifted composer as Jerry Goldsmith. I will not mention the remake or Marc Streitenfeld's music in this review.

*Poltergeist* is a Jerry Goldsmith movie, and we should think of *Poltergeist* as one of his best scores. The reason I have included this review in my book is that in the popular *Carol Anne's Theme* we have one of Goldsmith's most beautiful themes, but with his music for the horror scenes perhaps one of the finest examples of terrific horror scoring in modern cinema as well.

### The movie

*Poltergeist* was directed by Tobe Hooper, the director of *The Texas Chain Saw Massacre* (1974), one of the most influential modern horror movies. Because of the splatter context of that movie, it is hard to believe that *Poltergeist* is a Tobe Hooper movie.

The producer was Steven Spielberg, and as he had a clause in his contract preventing him from directing another movie while he made *E.T.* (1982), Hooper was selected. I do not want to mention the creative credit argument further here because this is not the place for it.

In the liner notes to the CD, Jon Burlingame assumes that the closest antecedent of the movie may have been an episode from Rod Serling's classic TV series *The Twilight Zone* called *Little Girl Lost* (1962), written by the renowned Richard Matheson about a child who falls into another dimension and has to be traced by her parents.[54] *Poltergeist* is more of a scary ghost than that TV episode. The movie starts with some satirical comments about the typical American middle-class family, then slowly lets the suspense rise with the first appearance of the ghosts, before soon getting scarier until the over-the-top horror showdown ultimately with huge amounts of special effects.

Steven Spielberg said about the movie that it was the "darker side of my nature when I was scaring my younger sister to death. In *Poltergeist* I wanted to terrify, and I also wanted to amuse – I tried to mix the laughs and the screams together." [55]

The movie was so successful that other films in the *Poltergeist* franchise were produced. For the second one, Jerry also wrote the music, but I will concentrate on the first one here. The film was a major critical and commercial success, being the eighth highest-grossing film of 1982. There is also a weird story about a *Poltergeist* curse because of the death of several people associated with the film, but I think that is just a marketing story like *The Omen* curse.

## The music

*Poltergeist* would be a great movie for any composer, but it was perfect for Jerry Goldsmith who like Bernard Herrmann also worked on *The Twilight Zone*. The plot gave the composer plenty of chances for his artificial composing style. Therefore, *Poltergeist* shows the whole range of Goldsmith's ability to write film music. There are lovely tracks such as *Carol Anne's Theme*, but also the typical atonal and modern music in the action tracks and scary music Goldsmith is famous for.

It is astonishing how Goldsmith develops his material, guides the audience on this musical journey and scares the hell out of them in the horror scene. I remember seeing the now famous clown scene in the movie, and it is Goldsmith's effective music that drives the scenes and scares the audience.

As I read in the liner notes, Spielberg contacted Goldsmith five months before the film went into production. Tobe Hooper was not involved with postproduction, so Spielberg and Goldsmith sat down together to discuss the musical approach. Goldsmith explained: "Anything I did was not of my own volition; it was a joint effort in that we both agreed what we were trying to do with the music for the picture. We wanted a childlike theme for the little girl. Steven felt that much of the action in the closet should have a quasi-religious atmosphere to it."

An excellent example of this is the track *Rebirth* for one of the best scenes. This track is one of the best tracks Goldsmith ever composed and stunning in its dramaturgical structure.

In the liner notes to the 1982 *Poltergeist* soundtrack, producer Steven Spielberg wrote some very kind words about the composer: "I have been an admirer of Jerry Goldsmith from the moment I heard his score for *The Blue Max* and *A Patch of Blue*. Along with John Williams, these two men have dominated the arena of great movie music for nearly 20 years. [...] Now with *Poltergeist*, Jerry has met his greatest challenge – to scare us nearly to tears, and he has been remarkable in his effort. Cleverly, the moments of greatest tension arise not from his brilliant off-rhythm, ostinatos but more from a soothing tonal beauty. Don't trust the melodies. Something perfectly unworldly is due to occur the moment you let your guard drop and Goldsmith proceeds to feign and attack with no 'apparent' rhyme or pattern."

The main theme is a lullaby called *Carol Anne's Theme*, a lovely theme to represent the quiet and peaceful life in this suburban area. Carol Ann is also the name of the little girl who has the first connection with the ghost and subsequently gets sucked into the ghost world. This main theme was part of the movie theme suite Goldsmith conducted during his concert tours, and it is one of the most beautiful love themes he composed.

Despite this lovely theme, Goldsmith created a lot of dissonant and atonal music for the horror scenes. It is astonishing how Goldsmith succeeds in switching between the more lyrical parts of the movie and the terror parts, which need a score to increase the horror parts. As John Williams was tied into *E.T.*, Spielberg turned to Goldsmith, and we can be glad that these two movies were made at the same time otherwise Goldsmith might not have been hired to compose the score for *Poltergeist*.

The score undertakes the same journey as the audience in the movie. First, it starts with the lyrical and quieter part of the music, then it transfers to a more richly orchestrated part of the score with a motif that some critics describe as the "religious theme" and which you can hear in the above-mentioned *Rebirth*. In the end, there are the scary parts of the score for the horror scenes, not an easy-listening part of the score. There are some similarities between these parts and the mystic parts of the first *Indiana Jones*, especially the temple scenes. Perhaps Spielberg asked Goldsmith to compose the music in a similar style?

*Escape from Suburbia* is a good example of these atonal and dissonant horror tracks. After the horror is over and the family is safe in a motel – the TV set will not stay in this room… – Goldsmith returns to more lyrical times with a reprise of *Carol Anne's Theme*, but he puts some children's laughter in at the end. This sounds weird and is unexpected. Is this a musical statement for the madness that still might be there?

Goldsmith did not use any synthesisers or electronic effects in the score. Instead, like in *Planet of The Apes*, he uses traditional instruments but also a lot of other instruments such a musical saw, a rub rod, whistles and drums to create the unknown in music. Even though the music for the showdown is not easy-listening music and people might skip this track, you have to admire Goldsmith's ability to transform the scary scenes into outstanding music.

These qualities make *Poltergeist* special and one of the best soundtracks ever: there are the lovely tracks, but also the musical horror scaring you with their unusual orchestration. Goldsmith showed again that he is a master in the horror genre.

After being unreleased for nearly fifteen years, *Poltergeist*'s first soundtrack album came out in 1997 on the Rhino Movie Music label. In 2010, a two-disc soundtrack album followed with Film Score Monthly featuring additional source and alternate material.

It is sad that Goldsmith and Spielberg did not work more together because Spielberg's genius at visual storytelling is perfectly matched with Goldsmith's genius for musical storytelling. *Poltergeist* is not only a great score, but shows that film music can be contemporary music that can be played unchanged in a concert hall.

## 42. CINDERELLA – THE PERFECT FAIRY TALE SCORE

I have to say I was not particularly interested in seeing this new *Cinderella* movie. When my friend asked me if I wanted to join her for a movie and suggested *Cinderella*, I was not very excited, but then I checked the facts: Kenneth Branagh was its director and Patrick Doyle its composer, as is nearly always the case when Branagh directs a movie. That sounded interesting!

**The movie**

*Cinderella* is a 2015 American romantic fantasy film directed by Kenneth Branagh, with the screenplay written by Chris Weitz. The film is based on the folktale and inspired in part by Walt Disney's 1950 animated film. The film stars the gorgeous Lily James as Cinderella, Richard Madden as the charming prince, and Cate Blanchett as the cruel stepmother. Helena Bonham Carter makes a fabulous appearance as Fairy Godmother.

Even though I was initially not so keen to see it, I was immediately captivated by it. Let's face it: this movie is excellent! A beautiful example of how a fairy tale should be directed these days. The special effects are perfectly integrated into the story, and it just fun to see the actors playing their roles. They seemed to have as much fun performing it as I was having watching it. Cate Blanchet is marvellous as the evil stepmother. I did not like her performance as the antagonist in the last *Indiana Jones*, but here she is great. Richard Madden is a charming prince, and Lily James is the perfect Cinderella.

*Cinderella* had its world premiere on 13 February 2015 at the 65th Berlin International Film Festival and was released in cinemas on 13 March 2015. It grossed over $543 million worldwide, becoming Branagh's highest-grossing film to date as a director, and received mostly positive reviews. The film received an Academy Award nomination for Best Costume Design at the 88th Academy Awards.

After the release and success of *Cinderella*, along with *Maleficent* (2014, with a fantastic score by James Newton Howard), *The Jungle Book* (2016) and *Beauty and the Beast* (2017), Walt Disney Pictures has announced the development of several other live-action remakes from their animated classics series. Perhaps an opportunity for Patrick Doyle to bring back romance and fantasy?

**The music**

And now for Patrick Doyle's music. I do not want to say that his music is the best part of the movie because that would give the impression that the film is not worth seeing. I highly recommend seeing it! We chose an afternoon to watch it, and it was so much fun having kids around who are enjoying the movie, the funny special effects, the humour and the romance.

This kind of movie is perfect for Patrick Doyle. It gives the composer plenty of chances to develop melodies and a lovely atmosphere. For me, this is Doyle's best soundtrack in recent years. I liked how he developed his melodies, especially the tracks using the piano (e.g. *Ella and Kit*). They are very touching.

Branagh knows about the importance of Doyle's music: "The tone we were trying to achieve was playful and joyful, but also emotional without being manipulative. Patrick found a beautiful yet robust tune that could be orchestrated so that it could offer lots of moods. It had simplicity, joy, and added a sense of fun. And, of course, his trademark: romantic." [56]

With 30 tracks – three of them are songs – you get a lot of music for your money, and the score is highly enjoyable. I want to give some recommendations and comment on some of the highlights in this score. While listening to the first track, you will immediately fall in love with this score. The soundtrack, played by the London Symphony Orchestra, debuted at No. 60 on the Billboard 200, selling 8,000 copies in its first week.

Track 5 *The First Branch* is the first highlight with Doyle using the piano. The usage of this instrument reminded me of raindrops falling. *The Stag* (track 8) is Doyle at his best: the composer uses the full force of the orchestra and develops a fantastic dramaturgical structure. Turn the speakers up loud for this track! *Fairy Godmother* (track 10) is a highly enjoyable scene in the movie, and so is the music. Doyle uses a mixture of strings and choir to create a magical atmosphere. The funny tune continues with *Pumpkins and Mice* (track 11). Here pizzicato strings start before the full orchestra enters.

One of my favourite tracks is *La Valse De L'Amour* (track 15). Patrick Doyle said in an interview that he started by writing the grand waltz that is the movie's centrepiece, as Cinderella charms the prince and the King's court at a lavish ball at the palace. "Everything leads to the ballroom and beyond," Doyle explains, "so it was crucial." Therefore, this waltz is exactly as it has to be: "simple and direct, but with strength."

This main waltz might motivate you to go back to dance classes and improve your own waltz skills. What a charming scene in the movie, what a lovely melody! Track 19 *The Secret Garden* underscores the scene when the bell is ringing and Cinderella has to leave. Doyle first develops a haunting atmosphere, and you can also hear the sound of the bell, and then the drama starts and the music erupts.

My favourite track is *Pumpkin Pursuit* (track 22). This is an energetic, powerful track, full of speed and action. The orchestra is on fire to underscore the dramatic scene of Cinderella's escape. This 2'30 track is so enjoyable that you want to hear it again and again.

After that, *The Slipper* (track 23) and *Shattered Dreams* (track 24) are quieter ones and focus more on the romantic moments. *Ella and Kit* (track 26) I have already mentioned. *Courage and Kindness* (track 27) is the last orchestral piece of the score and a fantastic ending to this highly enjoyable soundtrack.

For me, this score is the perfect fairy tale, and it shows how much romance, energy and drama a very gifted composer can bring to one soundtrack when the inspiration flows thanks to having a beautifully balanced movie to work on.

## 43. STAR TREK BEYOND – A STAR TREK FOR THE NEXT GENERATION

This second and last review of a score by Michael Giacchino in my book was a hard one to choose. I attended his 50th birthday celebration concert on Friday 20 October 2017 at the Royal Albert Hall in London. I learnt that as a little kid Michael drew pictures of the Enterprise spaceship and was a big fan of Spider-Man.

This concert was a big celebration in tribute to Michael Giacchino's video games, TV and feature movies he has done in recent years. It was not only a pleasure to listen to his music, conducted by the fabulous conductor Ludwig Wicki and some tracks by Giacchino himself, but it was also heart-warming to listen to host Adam Savage and guests such as J.J. Abrams, *Rogue One* director Gareth Edwards, *Up* director Pete Doctor and *John Carter* director Andrew Stanton praise Giacchino's talent, personality and music. What a great evening! Stanton showed a great sense of humour when he asked the audience who had actually seen *John Carter* (2012) and some cheers were heard. I have to admit I was not one of them…

Michael Giacchino is becoming really popular these days and has composed for nearly every big franchise. He is the composer of the new *Star Trek* movies, composed the music for *Rogue One* (2016), replacing Alexandre Desplat who was no longer able to do it, created the music for *Spider-Man: Homecoming* (2017) and for *Dawn of the Planet of the Apes (2014) and War for the Planet of the Apes* (2017) after Patrick Doyle composed the music for *Rise of the Planet of the Apes* (2011). For the music for Pixar's *Up* (2009), as already mentioned Giacchino was awarded an Oscar.

There are so many soundtracks to mention that I was struggling to pick one. Eventually, I decided to write about *Star Trek Beyond* (2016) just because of the track *A Night on the Yorktown*.

### The movie

I am still not a big fan of 3D movies in general – in my opinion it is just another way to make more money through increased ticket prices. You can watch most movies in 2D and have plenty of fun. A good story does not typically need 3D, and in most cases the films have been shot in 2D and just converted to 3D, which is evident.

I remember seeing Martin Scorsese's *Hugo* (2011), and the 3D was amazing because Scorsese knew how to use the technique correctly. When watching *Star Trek Beyond*, I was only astonished by what computer effects these days can achieve. This scene when the Enterprise approaches the Yorktown and the effects of this city in space are amazing!

*Star Trek Beyond* is the thirteenth film in the Star Trek franchise and the third movie in the reboot series. Chris Pine and Zachary Quinto reprise their roles, with Anton Yelchin in the role for Chekov. Unfortunately, he died shortly after finishing the movie, and as a sign of respect, no new actor will take over his role. Simon Pegg repeated his role as Scotty and was also co-author of the script.

For me, it was interesting that two of the long-awaited blockbusters that season used the idea of a swarm, the sequel to *ID4* and this *Star Trek* movie. Even though, I still prefer the original *Star Trek* series because of the cast, the old 60s charm and the sometimes great story-telling, the new *Star Trek* movies are good. This one in particular is better than the last one because I was so disappointed by Benedict Cumberbatch's performance as Khan. Ricardo Montalbán had been perfect in the role and gave a tremendous performance in this personification of Friedrich Nietzsche's superman concept.

**The music**

The soundtrack to this new *Star Trek* movie was also one of the most awaited that year. It was the second Giacchino soundtrack I bought and I really enjoy listening to it. Giacchino demonstrates what a gifted composer he is by developing his melodies and using the full force of the orchestra.

The first track *Logo and Prosper* is one of the highlights. I like its dark tone and the percussion before we hear the theme for the reboot series. The next highlight is just the second track *Thank Your Lucky Star Date*; the use of the piano in this track reminds me of Jerry Goldsmith's last soundtrack for the franchise.

And then, surprise, surprise, the third track offers the next highlight and the best track of the whole score: *Night on the Yorktown*. This is the second longest piece, and I kept listening to it over and over again. It is an epic piece of music, with a wonderfully developed dramaturgy. The choir might be a little bit too much, but for me, this is definitely the best track on the CD!

The next tracks take us towards the action scenes. Track 5 *A Swarm Reception* is a typical Giacchino action track. I still miss a straightforward action approach in the composition of these tracks; sometimes I think his way of composing and the way these tracks are orchestrated are a little bit too complex. Track 6 *Hitting the Saucer a Little Hard* is the longest track. Again, an action track, and again Giacchino uses the full power of the orchestra. On screen, this music has a tremendous effect. After the Enterprise is attacked, the track slows down with a more lyrical part.

Out of the following tracks, I have not found a real highlight to listen to more often. Sometimes I think the music is a little bit too noisy, and I miss a second powerful theme that could carry the second half of the score. To mention a few of the next tracks: track 7 *Jaylah Damage* is interesting because of the percussion, track 10 *A Lesson in Vulcan Mineralogy* is nice because of the flute in the last minute, and track 11 *Motor Cycles of Relief* is another action track in the typical busy Giacchino style, perhaps the best action track of the score. Therefore, I mostly skip the action tracks when I listen to it. I like track 17 *Par-tay for the Course* because of the piano part at the beginning.

Overall, I recommend buying this score for the first three tracks; the others are a matter of taste. When I listen to Giacchino's action tracks, I feel that he is highly skilled as a composer, but perhaps his tracks are too busily orchestrated.

Anyway, Giacchino is one of the best composers of film music these days, and his ability to compose richly orchestrated music for nearly every franchise in the last few years will guarantee him a place among the best film music composers ever.

## 44. Raiders of the Lost Ark – The most famous film music march

When selecting the soundtracks, I wanted to review in this book, I had to make choices. One choice was to skip John Williams's *Star Wars* soundtracks. Why the hell did I want to do it? They are iconic, they are marvellous, and they are one of the best examples of well-known film music! Yes, that is exactly right, and because we all know this, I decided to skip them. What else could I tell my readers about these scores that they already did not know?

Instead, I decided to talk about *Raiders of the Lost Ark* (1981). Of course, these are as popular as the *Star Wars* scores, but in my opinion, with the music for the first *Indiana Jones* movie, John Williams composed his best soundtrack for a franchise. I will explain in the next few pages why I think this.

### The movie

The first movie in the *Indiana Jones* franchise was the result of George Lucas's intention to create a modern version of the serials of the 1930s and 1940s he watched as a kid on Saturday afternoons. These series had a very straight forwarded storytelling style and each episode ended with a cliffhanger, a scene showing the main character facing a very dangerous situation he had to escape from, e.g. he was confronted by a number of bad guys, lost his weapons, fell into a trap, was locked in a room with a bomb in it etc.

The idea of these cliffhangers was to make sure that the audience returned to see how the hero survived this difficult situation. When I watched these serials as a kid, I recognised that the producers sometimes cheated. In the next episode we could see some things that made it possible for the hero to escape, and these tiny little changes in the setting had not been apparent the week before.

*Raiders of the Lost Ark* is a 1981 American action-adventure film directed by Steven Spielberg, with a screenplay written by Lawrence Kasdan, from a story by George Lucas and Philip Kaufman. Harrison Ford plays the archaeologist Prof. Henry Jones, who soon finds himself fighting a group of Nazis who are searching for the Ark of the Covenant, which Adolf Hitler believes will make his army invincible.

The film co-stars Karen Allen as Indy's former lover Marion Ravenwood and who returned for the fourth movie and eventually married Henry Jones Jr. Paul Freeman plays Indiana's rival, the French archaeologist René Belloq, John Rhys-Davies gives an entertaining performance as Indiana's sidekick Sallah, Ronald Lacey is unbelievable good as the sadistic Gestapo agent Arnold Toht, who is shockingly killed in the end, and Denholm Elliott gives his first performance as Indiana's colleague Marcus Brody, playing the typical stereotype of an academic lecturer who has trouble surviving in the real world.

The first movie is perhaps the best in the whole franchise. The sequel is unnecessarily violent, and the fourth is not a good movie overall and left fans disappointed. With Sean Connery playing Indiana Jones's father, the third one is by far the most entertaining of the series. The showdown in *Raiders* scared the hell out of me when I saw it as a teenager, especially the face melt scene, but the opening scene as well... my God, I hate these big spiders!

*Raiders of the Lost Ark* opened at #14 and grossed $1,673,731 during its opening weekend. The film, made on an $18 million budget, grossed $384 million worldwide and was the highest-grossing film of 1981 in the US. It remains one of the top twenty-five highest-grossing films ever made when adjusted for inflation.

## The music

When composing the music for this movie, I am sure John Williams had no idea that he was writing the music for the next big franchise with which his name would become closely associated. The *Raiders* march is one of the most popular themes in movie history, and like the Imperial March from *Star Wars*, the *Superman* theme, the theme for *Jaws* or more recently the *Harry Potter* theme, yet another iconic theme composed by Williams.

If you compare all four soundtracks to the *Indiana Jones* movies, I think the first one is the best. What I like is the haunting atmosphere, similar to John Williams's music for *Dracula* or *The Fury*, which I have also discussed in this book.

My favourite track is *The Map Room Down*. It is a perfect example of how to underscore a movie scene. The piece starts slowly with the haunting theme, then builds up the suspense, and when the sun finally comes out and shows Indy the way to the Ark, the orchestra opens up and the music finally erupts. When you listen to this music, you immediately have the scene in your mind. This track is definitely one of the best tracks Williams has ever composed.

There are different versions of this soundtrack, so I will not mention the track listing here. The CD I have has 19 tracks and begins with *The Raiders March*. If you compare this soundtrack with the next Indiana Jones scores, then this music is the most modern in its manner of composition. In the liner notes, Williams describes the *Raiders March* as hard work to come up with finally: "A piece like that is deceptively simple to try to find the few right notes that will make a right leitmotivic identification for a character like Indiana Jones. I remember working on that thing for days and days, changing notes, changing this, inverting that, trying to get something that seemed to me to be right. I can't speak for my colleagues but for me things which appear to be very simple are not at all, they're only simple after the fact. The manufacture of these things which seem inevitable is a process that can be laborious and difficult." [57]

Some tracks are very dependent on the dramatic structure of the film, e.g. *Main Title: South America, 1936* when Indiana Jones is introduced. It is a fabulous scene, and I wish that Spielberg had created a scene like this for the fourth movie when Indy finally appears on screen after such a long wait.

The next track *In the Idol's Temple* is astonishingly orchestrated. Listen to the way Williams underscores the scene when Jones discovers the spiders. Williams then builds up the haunting atmosphere perfectly and creates suspense until Indy finally stands in front of the golden statue. The music then switches immediately to action when Indy must escape. A perfect piece of music!

In *Journey to Nepal* we hear the wonderful love theme for the first time (longer and better further on in the track *Marion's Theme*), but here it is immediately interrupted by the theme for the Ark. I do not want to comment on every track, so let's mention *The Basket Game* as another example of the typical funny tracks in the scherzo style that Williams is famous for. Remember the scene when Indy shoots the master swordsman in the middle of the track? *Airplane Fight* and *Desert Chase* are good examples of Williams's action writing, with its dominant focus on the brass section to underscore the military aspects of the movie.

In the liner notes Williams wrote: "I always approach those things particularly with Steven in sort of balletic terms. I look at it as a kind of musical number that has a beginning, a middle and an end, and try to calculate a series of tempos, and a series of changing tempos. I will try to design it in almost in the same way as you would a balletic number, which may contribute a certain aspect of fun and adventurousness in this Harrison Ford character. The music may sound serious but it's not really, it's more theatrically conceived and hopefully always has an aspect of fun or even camp about it."

Before we have the music for the showdown, the track *Art Trek* gives us another strong performance of the haunting Ark theme. *The Miracle of The Ark* underscores the shocking finale with its amazing special effects. Williams transforms the whole magical atmosphere into music and underscores the shocking effects with harsh and nearly brutal orchestral attacks.

This kind of violent music is typical of early Williams's soundtracks, and therefore I like these scores much better than his later ones. The music for the death of the Nazis is as close to contemporary classical music as Williams has ever produced. The last minute brings this piece to a majestic ending, again with the Ark theme. *The Warehouse* and *End Credits* bring the soundtrack to an end.

It can be argued whether *Raiders of the Lost Ark* is Steven Spielberg's best action movie, but its score is definitely the most astonishing in Williams's whole career. He has never been better, and for me this score tops even his *Star Wars* soundtracks due to the perfect balance of romance and action, but primarily because of the harshness of the musical approach.

## 45. Under Fire – There are no pan-flutes in Nicaragua...

Jerry Goldsmith's *Under Fire* (1983) occupies a unique place in my heart. I was fortunate to see this movie in a cinema in my small hometown, the first movie with a score by Jerry that I had ever seen at the cinema. Since discovering Jerry Goldsmith in 1989, I have tried to watch every movie with his music in it in a big cinema.

Seeing Jerry Goldsmith's name on a big movie screen has been a heart-warming experience on each occasion. After I read about his cancer diagnosis, I was never sure whether the Jerry Goldsmith movie I was watching would be the last one I would ever see with his music in it. This was finally the case with *Looney Tunes: Back in Action* (2003).

### The movie

*Under Fire* is an American political thriller film set in the last days of the Nicaraguan Revolution that ended the Somoza regime in 1979. It stars Nick Nolte, Gene Hackman and Joanna Cassidy. Jerry Goldsmith's score featured well-known US jazz guitarist Pat Metheny and was nominated for an Academy Award. The film editing by Mark Conte and John Bloom was nominated for a BAFTA Award for Best Editing, and the film was shot in the Mexican states of Chiapas and Oaxaca.

Nick Nolte gives one of the best performances in his career and I think it is also Roger Spottiswoode's best movie. The director, who also worked as a cutter for legendary director Sam Peckinpah, became more famous for his Bond movie *Tomorrow Never Dies* (1997), Arnold Schwarzenegger's *The Sixth Day* (2000) and Sylvester Stallone's comedy disaster *Stop! Or My Mom Will Shoot* (1992), but *Under Fire* is the best movie of his career and his most critically well-received.

Even though the film is fictional, it was inspired by the murder of ABC reporter Bill Stewart and his translator Juan Espinoza by National Guard forces on 20 June 1979. ABC cameraman Jack Clark was shooting "incidental" footage and caught the entire episode on tape. The footage was shown on national television in the United States and became a major international incident, undermining what remained of dictator Anastasio Somoza's support. The incident was the final straw for the Carter Administration's relationship with Somoza, whose regime fell on 19 July (this explains one of the score's track title). Nolte's character is based on Matthew Naythons who was a photojournalist in Nicaragua and consultant during the shooting of *Under Fire*.

## The music

In the liner notes, Roger Spottiswoode praised Jerry Goldsmith's famous score for *Patton*: "Several years ago I went to a screening of *Patton* and came away immensely impressed with a splendid film. George C. Scott's extraordinary performance, the fine script and breath-taking scope of the direction had added up to a real work of art. But perhaps more than these, Jerry Goldsmith's memorable score has remained vivid ever since. He expressed the inner dreams and complexities of a severely private man, while illuminating the vulnerability of a soldier driven to realize his own mythology. In spite of the scale of the battles, he was always able to focus our emotions onto the plight of the individual soldiers and into Patton himself. There was always great sentiment but never sentimentality"[58] – a pretty good summary of Goldsmith's way of composing.

The classic WWII movie *Patton* (1970) and the Nicaragua movie *Under Fire* seem first not have much in common, but if you read these notes from Spottiswoode, there are see similarities between these two "war" movies. The director pointed further out: *Under Fire* is also "about the war itself. From the inception of Ron Shelton's screenplay, I felt that Jerry Goldsmith would be able to illuminate the complexities of the moral choices facing the characters while at the same time taking us musically into the heart of a revolution. His score takes us on an emotional voyage into a foreign would and makes it real and accessible. It suggests that in spite of all that has been written and said, finally the issues are very human, very painful, very sad. [...] He brought to the film not only his customary fine artistry, but also, and most importantly, great humanity." [59]

After these precise words about the musical approach, it is difficult to write anything myself about the score. For *Under Fire*, Goldsmith combined electronics and the orchestral sound again and used a great many solo instruments, such as pan flutes for the Central American setting and the guitar played by Metheny.

The composer pointed out to the studio that the temp track used in the film with the pan flute was not appropriate to the region, but he had to use the instruments for the score. In the liner notes Spottiswoode praised these instruments as being the heart of the score, but Goldsmith was aware that pan flutes were not right for the setting. At one of Goldsmith's concerts I went to at the Barbican in London, the composer talked about this episode. After one concert in which the music was played, one guy from the audience went up to him afterwards and said: "You know they don't use pan flutes in Nicaragua!", and Goldsmith made a sarcastic comment about this experience.

In the musical approach he took, *Under Fire* is one of Goldsmith's best scores. Jazz guitarist Pat Metheny fell ill during recording and had to record his solo parts a few days later. Metheny's way of playing fits perfectly with the score and its lyrical and folk music approach.

Goldsmith used four themes in this score. The most lyrical one is *Rafael's Theme*, also used as the love theme in the track *A New Love*. The composer also added synthesisers to the score brilliantly, for example in the track *Rafael*. There is then a march and a victorious rebel theme that can be heard in *19 de Julio*, a track with heavy use of synthesisers. Another theme is known as *Alex's Theme* (track 9).

The first track called *Bajo Fuego* is the best track of the whole score. Goldsmith combines the solo guitar played by Metheny and the orchestra perfectly. I remember a very nice situation when I was listening to the album at home. My mother came into my room and really liked the second track *Sniper*, particularly the way in which Goldsmith created a lovely atmosphere in the first few seconds of the track before the shocking outburst of the music when the murder takes place. How Goldsmith was then able to return to the lovely atmosphere with the orchestra, pan pipes, guitar and further percussion is genuinely a sign of how gifted this composer was.

The score is highly enjoyable in the different way Goldsmith uses his themes. After the dramatic *Sniper* track, there is a very lyrical one with *House of Mammocks*, then in track 4 *Betrayal* a more dramatic one, one of the best of the score.

Track 6 *Rafael* is indeed a masterpiece in the way Goldsmith composed this track for one of the most important scenes of the movie. You can see what a photograph is able to do! This track again combines the orchestra and the pan flutes, with the military march now becoming more dominant. It is another highlight of the score, and even without seeing the movie it is possible to imagine what is happening. This is musical storytelling at its best!

After the more lyrical *A New Love,* the pan flutes dominate the next track *Sandino* before we have another lyrical track called *Alex's Theme* (which I normally skip). Then we have the lovely *Fall of Managua. Rafael's Theme* is the track featuring local folk music the most in the whole score. Guitar, pan flutes and the orchestra work perfectly together. I especially love the last minute of this track.

The last one *Nicaragua* is like a summary of all the different aspects of the score and the last highlight. This wonderfully composed and orchestrated track is one of my all-time favourites, and again fabulous musical story-telling. There are the folk elements first, then the dominance of the march and the military aspects, as if the music wants to tell you that innocent local people have been overrun by the military but are now finally returning to their peaceful lives.

*Under Fire* is still a movie worth watching, but it could be said that without Jerry Goldsmith's music this movie would perhaps not be as popular as it is. This score is not only an example of amazing movie music, but is also like film music should be: supporting the movie in the best way possible and standing alone as a true masterpiece.

# 46. THE MASK OF ZORRO – A RARE EXPERIENCE

What should my last review of a score by James Horner be in this book? One evening, I was standing with a nice glass of red wine in front of my CDs, picked one up, looked at it, put it back, then grabbed another one and so on: too many options to choose from.

When I started writing this book, I was very clear that it would not be *Titanic* (1997). Even though this score might be the most popular one by James Horner, it is by far not his best, and more typical in the way that a highly successful film just has an average score.

James Horner's idea of composing a song and putting it at the end was a brilliant idea, convincing Celine Dion to sing it even smarter, and putting this song only on the soundtrack album perhaps the smartest of all. Horner got an Academy Award for this score (and the song), highly deserved as a composer, but I do not think that *Titanic* is James Horner's best score.

So, what should the last James Horner review in this book be? I opted for *The Mask of Zorro* (1998) because it is one of the rare examples of an excellent movie also having an excellent score. The elegant main theme, the straightforward action tracks and the fantastic orchestration makes *The Mask of Zorro* one of James Horner's best scores and a CD I like to listen to a lot.

### The movie

*The Mask of Zorro* is a 1998 American swashbuckler film based on the character of the masked vigilante Zorro, created by Johnston McCulley (1883-1958), a former police officer who was the author of hundreds of stories, fifty novels and screenplays for film and television. McCulley's Zorro was reminiscent of Baroness Orczy's Scarlet Pimpernel and was first serialised in the story *The Curse of Capistrano* in 1919 in the pulp magazine *All-Story Weekly*.

Zorro became very popular, featured in four novels and appeared on screen in the silent movie *The Mark of Zorro* portrayed by Douglas Fairbanks. Rouben Mamoulian's 1940 version is also very popular, with Tyrone Power as Zorro and a wonderful score by Franz Waxman. After this movie, McCulley decided to bring Zorro back with new stories and produced new Zorro stories for every issue of *West Magazine*, 53 in all. Guy Williams became popular as the actor in Walt Disney's *Zorro* television series from 1957 with 78 episodes and four specials.

*The Mask of Zorro* was initially developed by Steven Spielberg for TriStar Pictures with directors Mikael Salomon and Robert Rodriguez, before Campbell signed up for it in 1996. Salomon cast Sean Connery as Don Diego de la Vega, while Rodriguez brought Banderas into the lead role. Connery dropped out and was replaced by Anthony Hopkins. For the love interest, Catherine Zeta-Jones played Elena, the infant daughter of Hopkins' character who grew up to become a beautiful woman.

New Zealand-born Martin Campbell was the right director for this movie, and when seeing it I was really surprised at how entertaining it was. Zorro is part of my childhood memories. I loved this character and dressed up as Zorro when I was a child. When I heard about the movie, I was suspicious about whether Zorro is a character for a new film or should just be buried as childhood memories.

Martin Campbell also directed two James Bond movies and brought the franchise back to life with a new actor in the leading role twice, with *Goldeneye* (1995) starring Pierce Brosnan and later with *Casino Royale* (2006) starring Daniel Craig. Campbell directed *The Mask of Zorro* as a highly entertaining mixture of action, old-fashioned style and a good sense of humour. By accepting to do this movie, Campbell turned down the chance to direct the James Bond movie *Tomorrow Never Dies* (1997) and so Roger Spottiswoode took over.

*The Mask of Zorro* incorporates specific historical events and people. Banderas's character is the fictional brother of Joaquin Murrieta, a real Mexican outlaw who was killed by the California State Rangers led by Harry Love (portrayed as Captain Harrison Love) in 1853. The confrontation in the movie takes place more than a decade earlier, in 1841. As in the movie, Harry Love also kept Murrieta's head in an alcohol-filled glass jar. The opening sequence is set in the aftermath of the Mexican War of Independence.

*The Mask of Zorro* was a critical and commercial success and therefore a sequel called *The Legend of Zorro* (2005) was released, again with Banderas and Catherine Zeta-Jones, again directed by Campbell and again with a score by James Horner. Even though it now lacked new ideas and originality, I still enjoyed watching it.

## The music

This is another movie that was perfect for James Horner. The composer created an elegant main theme, significantly composed orchestrated action tracks and used the romantic moments to write one of his most beautiful love themes. Again, he used his favourite instrument, the Japanese shakuhachi flute, and contrasted it with the various Latin instruments he used throughout the score. Horner composed a song for Marc Anthony and Australian singer Tina Arena called *I Want to Spend My Lifetime Loving You*, but compared to *My Heart Will Go On*, the song is average even though it reached #3 in the French singles chart and #4 in the Dutch singles chart.

The score was Horner's first score good score after *Titanic* – *Deep Impact* (1998) is rather disappointing – and even though you can hear the typical Horner mannerisms in it, I think *The Mask of Zorro* is a much better score than *Titanic*. The main theme is more beautiful, the action music is more energetic, and the score is more ambitious. Horner used a lot of Latin flavour with hand clapping, flamenco guitars and castanets. The first track called *The Plaza of Execution*, also one of longest tracks, is the first highlight.

Track 2 *Elena And Esperanza* is a quieter and more lyrical one, before track 3 *The Ride*, a shorter one presenting more Latin flavour with castanets again. For me, track 5 called *The Fencing Lesson* is one of the most enjoyable tracks to one of the most enjoyable scenes. I like how Horner uses hand clapping balanced with trumpet and guitar. Track 6 *Tornado in The Barracks* is another of the score's highlights, very enjoyable and energetic and with a good sense of humour. Horner at his best!

The percussion in track 10 *Stealing the Map* is reminiscent of the use of percussion in *Titanic*, and with the 13-minute track *Leave No Witnesses...* we already have the music for the showdown. Track 12 *Diego's Goodbye* underscores the last scene of the movie and brings the orchestral part of the album to a powerful ending.

*The Mask of Zorro* is without doubt one of Horner's best scores. Perhaps the sequel *The Legend of Zorro* is more advanced in its composing style, but you can decide this for yourself. Both scores are excellent examples of Horner's exceptional contribution to the world of film music: elegant music, beautiful themes, powerful action music and timeless in taking the best possible approach!

## 47. STAR TREK – A SPACE OPERA

When I started writing this book, I was pretty sure that I do not want to talk about John Williams's *Star Wars* soundtracks, and explained why when writing about *Raiders of the Lost Ark*, but I did want to write about Jerry Goldsmith's *Star Trek* (1979).

Jerry Goldsmith did not compose the music for all the *Star Trek* movies, he composed the music for the first move then took a long break and came back with the great score for *Star Trek: The Final Frontier* (1989), composed the wonderful theme for *Star Trek: Voyager* and then worked on the feature films of the Star Trek Next Generation crew: *Star Trek: First Contact* (1996, with his son Joel, and for me Jerry's best score for the franchise), *Star Trek: Insurrection* (1998) and *Star Trek Nemesis* (2002, the last movie with a Jerry Goldsmith score I saw at the cinema). These five scores make him the most hired composer of the franchise.

*Star Trek: The Motion Picture* is not only one of Jerry Goldsmith's best scores and one of the best SF soundtracks ever, but it also typical of Jerry Goldsmith in a number of ways: an astonishing score for a movie that did not convince critics and failed to achieve the cult status of *Star Wars* for example. Compared to *Superman*, *Star Trek* was more successful, but because of a dialogue-heavy storyline and lack of action scenes, fans like its sequel *The Wrath of Khan* (1982) more with its James Horner score.

### The movie

When the original television series was cancelled in 1969, Gene Roddenberry, the creator of *Star Trek*, got in touch with Paramount to continue the franchise with a feature film. The final success of the series convinced the studio to start working on the film in early 1975, but the studio was unconvinced by the various attempts. Steven Spielberg's success with *Close Encounters of the Third Kind* (1977) led Paramount to reconsider the idea of a *Star Trek* feature movie.

Director Robert Wise was assigned to direct the movie. Wise, winner of two Academy Awards, worked with Goldsmith on the classic *The Sand Pebbles* (1966) starring Steve McQueen, and directed the first adaptation of a Michael

Crichton novel called *The Andromeda Strain* (1971), still one of the best movies based on a book by this famous author.

How the script was developed and the final movie put together is a very complicated story that I do not want to summarise here. In my opinion, the plot is not convincing and lacks the quality of a big screen adventure; it is more the plot of a TV episode that has been extended to fit a 132-minute movie. Douglas Trumbull and John Dykstra were assigned to finish the special effects and 100 matte paintings were also used, provided by Richard Yuricich. Even though the original cast returned and the special effects were astonishing, the movie is not as entertaining as it should have been for the first feature movie by the *Star Trek* crew.

## The music

While researching the movie, I read that Gene Roddenberry had initially wanted Jerry Goldsmith to score *Star Trek*'s pilot episode, *The Cage*, but the composer was unavailable. When Wise signed on to direct, Paramount asked the director if he had any objection to using Goldsmith. Wise replied: "Hell, no. He's great!" Wise later considered his work with Goldsmith one of the best relationships he ever had with a composer[60].

Even though Goldsmith had three to four months to compose the music, I read that because of the time pressure, Alexander Courage (composer of the original *Star Trek* theme), who later became another orchestrator for Jerry alongside his friend and long-time orchestrator Arthur Morton, was hired to provide the arrangements and Fred Steiner, who contributed music for the original series, to write some cues.

On YouTube, there are numerous videos with background information. In one adorable one, you see the struggle of the Indian actor Persis Khambatta who played Ilia when she loses her beautiful hair for the role. One member of the crew even gives her a tissue when her tears start falling. I agree with one of the comments on this video: it is very strange after seeing her hairless now seeing her with hair – it is hard to imagine this actress with hair.

*Star Trek*, as the original series pointed out, is a series about discovery and exploring new worlds. Therefore the spaceship can be considered as a vehicle like a ship or a waggon for exploring new territory like people did in the Wild

West. Jerry Goldsmith's initial overblown main theme reminded Wise of sailing ships, but unable to articulate what he felt was wrong with the piece, the director recommended writing an entirely different piece[61]. Compared to the original theme, this new *Star Trek* theme is more elegant and more majestic, and during this collaboration with the franchise, Goldsmith created variations of this theme. I was lucky enough to attend one of Goldsmith's concerts at the Barbican in London where Goldsmith focused on the musical material for the *Star Trek* franchise and played nearly one full concert of just *Star Trek* music.

The importance of the score for the movie can be seen by the fact that a three-minute *Overture* was composed as an initial opening before the credits. For this track, Goldsmith used the *Ilia* theme, the movie's love theme. Alongside the famous main theme and the love theme, there is also the *Klingon* theme, which is thrilling because of the percussion effects. Goldsmith used a lot of electronic instruments for the score, for example the blaster beam, an electronic instrument four metres long created by musician Craig Huxley, who played a small role in an episode of the original. This blaster had steel wires connected to amplifiers fitted to the main piece of aluminium, and the instrument was played with an artillery shell. Goldsmith decided to use it for V'Ger's cues.

There are different album versions of the soundtrack, and I will focus on the 20th Anniversary Collector's Edition, a two-CD set with 18 tracks. The CD starts with *Ilia's Theme*, the score's love theme, a wonderfully romantic piece of music. Track 2 is the *Main Title* with the new theme and then immediately the famous *Klingon Battle* for the first attack by the cloud. This track is well known and very famous for the percussion effects in music.

I do not want to comment on all of the tracks that follow. My favourite is track 6 *The Enterprise*. If you see how Kirk looks at the Enterprise, you get the feeling that this music is also a kind of love music (from 2'40). It is one of the best examples of how to underscore a scene like this, a great piece of music with a perfect suspense line until the new spaceship finally appears at 3'59 with, of course, the music completely erupting here.

Track 7 *Leaving Drydock* continues with this approach and gives another excellent performance of the main theme. This scene is created like similar scenes in old swashbuckler movies when the ship finally leaves the harbour and reaches the open ocean to explore new adventures.

Half of the music on the album underscores the Enterprise flying into the cloud and doing research. It is therefore challenging to mention just one or two tracks because they work more like a suite and it is hard to separate them. One of my favourite ones is track 9 called *The Cloud* because I love the wind-like effects at the beginning. Goldsmith is marvellous here in building up tension and the space atmosphere using different orchestral instruments and combining them with the various electronic effects. That is just an astonishing piece of music! The following track *Vejur Flyover* is perhaps even better and uses this way of creating an atmosphere in a more developed way, however you also need to have the scenes in mind. Track 13 *Spock Walk* is highly entertaining because of the short action music when Spock switches on his power and enters the cloud.

With track 17 *A Good Start* and then the famous *End Title* the album comes to an end. I love the energy of this last track with its main theme that even after nearly 40 years still has the power to carry a whole new franchise. Compare this theme to Michael Giacchino's for the new franchise series, and you will know what I mean.

*Star Trek – The Motion Picture* is a classic SF picture, but because of its lack of humour and the philosophical overkill not my favourite in the franchise. *Star Trek – First Contact* (1996) is a much better movie and for me the best in the franchise because of its dark elements. *Star Trek IV – The Voyage Home* (1986) has perhaps too many environmental messages, but I love this movie because of the funny hospital scene and Leonard Rosenman's great music for it.

For *Star Trek – First Contact*, Jerry Goldsmith composed one of his finer scores in the latter years of his career, with help from his son Joel for the electronic parts. *Star Trek Nemesis* (2002) is in my opinion one of the weakest parts of the franchise. I was so looking forward to it but left the cinema highly disappointed. Nevertheless, the music is again a fantastic contribution by Jerry Goldsmith and the best part of the movie.

*Star Trek – The Motion Picture* is considered by some critics as the best score in the whole franchise. We all have our own opinion of this assessment, but three facts are definite: this score is one of Jerry Goldsmith's best scores, one of the best SF scores ever written, and one of the few scores that genuinely deserves to be called a masterpiece of modern film music composing.

# 48. Interstellar – A Homage to 2001

This is the third and final review of a Hans Zimmer soundtrack in this book. Some critics think that the movie is not Christopher Nolan's best movie, preferring the *Batman* trilogy, but I have to say that I like *Inception* and *Interstellar* more than the *Batman* films.

I watched *Interstellar* (2014) when I was living in San Francisco and can remember my astonishment when I saw the last scenes and the mind-blowing visuals effects Nolan created. This is the kind of movie you have to see in a large cinema and one you will never forget.

## The movie

*Interstellar* is an epic SF film directed, co-written and co-produced by Christopher Nolan. The movie stars Matthew McConaughey, Anne Hathaway and Nolan's regular movie actor Michael Caine. Set in a future in which humanity is struggling to survive, it follows a group of astronauts who travel through a wormhole in search of a new home for mankind.

I look forward to any new Christopher Nolan film. He is the only director of this generation who can really tell a story in a mind-blowing movie experience every time. I always feel exhausted after watching a Nolan movie, especially the later ones. Nolan's films are so full of emotion and great scenes that you keep thinking of the visuals after seeing it, for example the Paris scenes in *Inception* and the bookshelves scenes in *Interstellar*.

Of course, this movie is a homage to SF classics such as Stanley Kubrick's *2001 – A Space Odyssey* (1968), perhaps also Fritz Lang's silent movie masterpiece *Metropolis* (1927) and other SF classics such as *Blade Runner* (1982), *Star Wars* (1977) and *Alien* (1979), which might have inspired the production design.

I do not want to talk here about the different SF topics in the movie, e.g. the time travel and its physical and logical aspects. There are many articles from much more sophisticated people than me who can explain you the possibility of these various aspects. For me, *Interstellar* is a very personal movie, perhaps Nolan's most personal film so far. It is a movie about love, more specifically about the love for the people we love, and especially how much we need our family and how sad we feel when we are separated from them.

## The music

Having got rather tired of the usual overblown music found in the latest Hans Zimmer soundtracks, I was really impressed by his music for this film. In an interview with Hollywood Reporter, the composer discussed the intense collaboration with Christopher Nolan and his ideas for the music. In the liner notes to the *Interstellar* CD, Nolan explained his "radical new approach"[62] with this movie.

He asked Hans Zimmer "to give me one day of his time. I'd give him an envelope with one page – a page explaining the fable at the heart of the movie-to-be. Hans would open the envelope, read it, start writing and at the end of the day he'd play me whatever he'd accomplished. That would be the basis of the score."[63] Therefore Hans Zimmer "took me at my word, and several months later, he gave me my day, forcing me to start my own creative journey by sitting down to write out my page."[64] Later that day, the composer called the director and played a simple piano melody that went directly to Nolan's heart and worked as the emotional guide. This track was called *Day One*.[65]

Zimmer had composed a four-minute piece for piano and organ: "I really just wrote about what it meant to be a father. And Nolan came down and sat on my couch, and I played it for him. He goes, 'Well, I better make the movie now'. And I'm going, what is the movie? And he starts describing this huge journey, this vast canvas of space and philosophy and science and all these things. And I'm going, 'Hang on. I've written you this tiny little thing here.' And he goes, 'Yes, but I now know what the heart of the story is'. So, he was writing with this piece of music sort of keeping him company all the way through the writing process, all the way through the shoot. At the end of the filming of *Interstellar*, Nolan gave Zimmer a watch. On the back it says, 'This is no time for caution,'"[66] said Zimmer.

In the liner notes to the CD, Hans Zimmer mentioned that it started with Christopher Nolan's idea of using a pipe organ this time. Even though I read that Zimmer had no idea that this movie would be an SF movie, the use of an organ reminds us of Kubrick's *2001* and the first notes of the fanfare of *Sunrise* from *Thus Spoke Zarathustra* by German composer Richard Strauss.

Richard Strauss composed this tonal poem inspired by Friedrich Nietzsche's philosophical book in which Nietzsche explained his ideas of the "Uebermensch" as a person who gives himself his own rules and fights against the obsolete morals of society.

Strauss's fanfare starts with a sustained double low C on the double bass, contrabassoon and organ. This transforms into the brass fanfare and introduces the "dawn" motif (from *Zarathustra's Prologue*, this motif includes three notes, at intervals of a fifth and an octave, as C–G–C). I listened to this piece during a concert in London's Royal Albert Hall, and the fanfare is still very impressive and powerful. Elvis Presley used it as the opening piece in his concerts between 1971 and 1977.

Using an organ for an SF movie might sound a little bit like a stereotype, but Zimmer used it not just for an opening track but made it an essential part of the whole score. Zimmer and Nolan visited London's Temple Church to record the 1926 four-manual Harrison & Harrison organ played by the church's music director Roger Sayer. Because of the use of the organ, this score by Hans Zimmer stands out among his recent works.

In the liner notes, Zimmer explains his early love for the organ as the most complex man-made musical device and his joy when he was finally old enough to reach the pedals. For this music, Nolan asked Zimmer not to use the big action drums or the propulsive string ostinato that the composer liked to use before.

Hans Zimmer started to synthesise sounds of air and wind to include in the music. Zimmer explained the exceptional process of the score when he composed and played the tracks, "with every note played solely by me"[67], and then Nolan and his team fit the music to the scene in the movie. Zimmer[68] mentioned that he never had the actual film in his studio to look at it while he wrote, an entirely unusual process compared to the other composers I have talked about in this book.

But Zimmer and Nolan had always planned an experimental music expedition to London to see what the "extraordinary musicians and the magnificent acoustics of two great churches could bring to the project".[69]

Zimmer's friend Richard Harvey suggested visiting Temple Church, and in the liner notes in a heart-warming way Zimmer explained his worries and then his astonishment at the organist Roger Sayer and his way of "taming the beast", Zimmer's nickname for the big organ.

The best music track of the score is the music to the *Docking Scene*. When I immediately went out after seeing the movie and bought the music album, now called the standard edition (with 16 tracks), this track was not on the album, and I had to download it via a link I found on Hans Zimmer's website. How could he not include this powerful music for one of the best scenes in the movie on the album?

The music has the right balance between the overblown pieces such as *Coward, Where We're Goin'* and *The Wormhole* with the organ and the more lyrical ones such as *Afraid of Time, Detach, I'm Going Home, S.T.A.Y* and *Stay* (perhaps the best two tracks after the music for the *Docking Scene* called *No Time for Caution*). There is one track called *Mountain* in which Zimmer uses a clock-like instrument and includes the typical clock ticking in the music as a musical concept of time.

I do not want to mention any more tracks from the album. The whole score has a good flow and typical of Zimmer in its musical approach. There are many more tracks that stand out other than the few I have mentioned. On the standard album I bought I missed the kind of end credits tracks that bring the album to a satisfying ending.

You also have to decide which album presentation you want to buy, and I do not understand why, other than for financial reasons, there is not just one album with all the essential cues on it.

For me, *Interstellar* is one of Zimmer's best works in recent years, even though it lacks a satisfying musical and dramaturgical structure. I still prefer his earlier and more theme-based soundtracks, but this music is exceptionally good on screen, and the track for the docking scene astonishingly good even when separated from the movie.

## 49. SOLO – A STAR WARS STORY – GETTING THE FLOW

While writing this book, another new *Star Wars* movie came out. Even though I still think the original trilogy will be the best *Star Wars* movies ever, I always look forward to a new one being released. It is astonishing how big the franchise has become, and I also think that the new *Star Wars* directors are creating better movies than George Lucas is with his own new films now.

As I explained before, I did not want to talk about John Williams's *Star Wars* soundtracks in this book, but I am having so much fun listening to John Powell's *Solo* that I decided to include a review of it in my book. Another reason is Powell's comments in an interview about the difficulties of writing a score like *Solo* these days. His statement perfectly sums up the issues in modern film music scoring.

### The movie

*Solo: A Star Wars Story* (2018), based on the character Han Solo and directed by Ron Howard, is the second *Star Wars* anthology film following 2016's *Rogue One*. I am starting to like these movies more than the "official" sequels. *Rogue One* was a very good war movie, while *Solo* is a good action movie with western elements and decent action scenes. The film stars Alden Ehrenreich as Han Solo, alongside Woody Harrelson, Emilia Clarke, Donald Glover and Paul Bettany.

George Lucas began the development in 2012 and asked Lawrence Kasdan to write the screenplay, which was completed by his son Jonathan after Kasdan was hired to write *Star Wars: The Force Awakens*. Kasdan is a fabulous writer and author of *The Empire Strikes Back* (with Leigh Brackett), *Raiders of the Lost Ark*, *Body Heat*, *Return of the Jedi* and *Silverado*, to mention just a few.

Principal photography began in January 2017 under the direction of Phil Lord and Christopher Miller. The pair left the project in June after being fired over "creative differences", and Ron Howard took over directing duties. With an estimated budget of at least $250 million, it is one of the most expensive films ever made and will need to gross $500 million to break even. On

Wikipedia, there is more information about what these "creative differences" were. It was reported that the directors were fired after Kennedy and Kasdan disagreed with their shooting style. Lord and Miller believed they were hired to make a comedy film, while Lucasfilm was looking to only add "a comedic touch".

I have read that Disney considers *Solo* a flop. I think there are three reasons for this. First, the Han Solo actor Alden Ehrenreich is just not as cool an actor as Harrison Ford and even though he tries his best with a nice smile, his constant remarks of "that'll be fun" or "no worries" are just annoying. George Lucas invented a large number of wonderful characters in *Star Wars*, but Solo might be his greatest achievement. Han Solo, possible the favourite character in the *Star Wars* universe, is a character everyone likes, considers as charming and can relate to despite him being a cynical pirate. And Ehrenreich? He is just the nice guy from the neighbourhood and a typical actor for today: nice, kind and, most of all, quite boring. Of course there will always be only one Harrison Ford, but perhaps you remember the bar scene from *The Intern* (2015). Anne Hathaway is going out with some of her colleagues and Robert De Niro is the intern. As the evening progresses, she gets drunk and then looks at her colleagues, typical hipsters, with frustration and complains: "How in one generation have men gone from guys like … Harrison Ford to…", and Hathaway looks at her colleagues. That is exactly the problem with today's generation of actors!

The second issue with *Solo* in my opinion is the typical trend of being politically correct. In an interview, Lando actor Donald Glover said Lando is a pan-sexual character. "How can you not be pansexual in space?" Glover said. "There's so many things to have sex with. I didn't think that was that weird. He's coming on to everybody. It just didn't seem that weird to me because I feel like if you're in space, it's kind of like the door's open … this thing is literally a blob. Like, 'Are you a man or a woman?' Who cares?" Glover's remarks are slightly different from Kasdan's own reasoning for announcing the character's sexuality. Kasdan told Huffington Post he wanted to bring more LGBTQ representation into the Star Wars universe, and wished he pressed a little more to have that representation visible in Solo. "There's a fluidity to Donald and Billy Dee's sexuality. I mean, I would have loved to have gotten a more explicitly LGBT character into this movie. I think it's time, certainly, for that, and I love the fluidity — sort of the spectrum of sexuality that Donald appeals to and that droids are a part of." [70]

People who want to see a new *Star Wars* movie do not much care about politically correct topics, especially not about bringing more LGBTQ representation into the *Star Wars* universe. *Star Wars* is a fairy tale and, as *Rogue One* showed us, can also be a war story, but is has nothing to do with being politically correct or discussing whether a character should have sex with a machine such as L3. In my opinion, most people are tired of this trend of always being politically correct, and that might be the reason why the first *Expendables* with Sylvester Stallone and the old action actors from the 1980s was such a success: it was just good old-fashioned entertainment!

A third reason may be its difficult production history. There was criticism that the directors were encouraging too much improvisation, which was believed to be "shifting the story off course" from the script. Lord and Miller also refused to compromise on certain scenes, such as filming a scene from fewer angles, thereby reducing the options available in editing.

Finally, Howard took over and re-shot nearly 70% of the film. Even though these differences cannot be seen on screen, I feel this is not a typical Ron Howard movie. If you compare this movie with *Ransom* (1996), *A Beautiful Mind* (2001), *The Da Vinci Code* (2006), *Frost/Nixon* (2008) or *Angels & Demons* (2009), there is a lack of good storytelling and a sense that Howard was not involved in the project from the outset. Anyway I had fun; the action scenes in particular are brilliantly filmed. Now let's talk about the music.

**The music**

In July 2017, John Powell was announced as the main composer of the score. John Williams composed and conducted the Han Solo theme on the CD called *The Adventures of Han*. Powell began writing the music in late 2017 and included Williams's new theme a great deal in his score, as well as Williams's music from previous films, most convincingly in the track *Reminiscence Therapy*, one of the best tracks on the CD.

Powell, born in 1963, learnt the violin as a child before studying at London's Trinity College of Music. He later went into jazz and rock music. After leaving college, he composed music for commercials, which led to a job as an assistant to the composer Patrick Doyle on several film productions, including *Much Ado About Nothing* (1993). Powell was a member of Hans Zimmer's music studio, Remote Control Productions, and has frequently collaborated with Harry Gregson-Williams and Zimmer himself.

My first CD with Powell's music was *Antz* (1998) and later I bought *Chicken Run* (2000), both highly enjoyable movies and scores. Powell was also responsible for the music for the *Shrek* movies, all with Gregson-Williams, and composed the music to John Woo's action classic *Face/Off* (1997, his first major film score), Ivan Reitman's mediocre SF action comedy *Evolution* (2001), Sylvester Stallone's *D-Tox Eye – See You* (2002, for me the worst Stallone movie ever), Matt Damon's *The Bourne Identity* (2002) and *How to Train Your Dragon* (2010, a very popular score), to name just a few.

Even though I like Michael Giacchino as a composer and have already discussed two of his soundtracks in this book, I did not buy his music for *Rogue One*. While watching the movie, I just could not get into the music. With Powell's music, it was different. I really liked his action tracks because they gave the movie the right drive, so I bought the CD and decided to discuss this music in my book here.

In an interview on YouTube, John Powell explains the difficulties of composing a score like this these days. He said that John Williams is "harmonically incredible fluid, it is polyphonic music, and nobody is doing this anymore". Most composers, he pointed out, are stuck now in the "keyboard player mode", and in Powell's opinion it is very hard to break out of this. He said the most important part was to get "flow". Williams's music is "always flowing forward; it is not just pulsing forward, like most of the score they have to do these days, it is flowing forward." To get a better idea of what Powel means, I suggest you listen to Hans Zimmer's action tracks from *Gladiator* and then to John Williams's *Star Wars* action tracks or John Powell's *Solo*, especially *Reminiscence Therapy*, and you will understand the difference in these two composing styles.

The CD has a huge number of fabulous action tracks. One of the highlights is *Corellia Chase*. I particularly love the music from 0'47 (strings part), which is wonderfully composed. This track is typical of most of the action pieces because the busy brass section reminds you of John Williams, but Powell increased the percussion section to give the music a very modern touch. Another highlight is *Flying with Chewie*; the title says it all.

*Meet Han*, the second track on the CD and the first original by Powell, is an epic track with sweeping strings and the typical special percussion arrangement that can be heard throughout the music. This fresh touch makes the CD so enjoyable! It is a short but epic track!

My favourite track is *Train Heist* for the best action scene in the movie. The track starts slowly, before the action starts at 1'30. The following seconds of music, brass combined with the percussion, is great action music. In my opinion the horn section should be a little bit louder.

The action continues with *Marauders Arrive* (another quieter moment in the middle of the track), before we have a song in a French chanson style with *Chicken in the Pot. Is This Seat Taken?* is good suspense (*Star Wars* theme for a few seconds). *L3 & Millennium Falcon* offer another example of just how perfectly Powell uses the various *Star Wars* themes in his score. The short *Lando's Closet* gives us a lyrical love theme for Lando.

The next two action tracks – *Mine Mission* and *Break Out* – are highly enjoyable and in the spirit of John Williams; even the brass section sounds familiar! As mentioned above, *Reminiscence Therapy* uses the Jedi theme even more effectively and some notes are copied from the music for the chase in the asteroid field from *The Empire Strikes Back*.

After listening to this music, I think John Powell would be the perfect person to continue the *Star Wars* saga. These tracks are exactly the kind of music I missed when listening to Giacchino's *Rogue One*! *Into The Maw* is the busiest action track of the score, with the orchestra on fire here!

*Testing Alliance* is a nice balanced piece between all the busy action music. The last track called *Dice & Roll* is more of a musical joke with its very modern way of using the Jedi theme and brings the album to an end. Unfortunately, it lacks end credit music.

John Powell's *Solo* is so enjoyable that it will be very difficult for any other composer to compete with his soundtrack this year. I did not expect very much of the music when I was buying my ticket for *Solo*, but I felt greatly entertained by the movie and especially by the music. Well done, John Powell!

## 50. Basic Instinct – Jerry Goldsmith's first and only erotic thriller

When I was coming to the end of writing this book, I thought about which film music the last review should cover. I was sure that it would be one of Jerry Goldsmith's scores, but which one? His score to *The Great Train Robbery* (1979) is one of my all-time favourites, and I love Michael Crichton's books and movies . So, should I talk about that one? But I also love the scores to the two *Gremlins* movies, which are classics, but which one?

Or perhaps the score to *Hoosiers* (1986) and the musical expression of dropping a basketball would be a good headline for the score... *King Solomon's Mines* (1985), one of the few later Goldsmith scores without electronics, might have been a good choice too. Or, *The Mummy* (1999), one of my favourite later scores by Goldsmith. So many choices, but there was only enough space for one.

I finally decided to choose *Basic Instinct* (1992), in my opinion one of Jerry Goldsmith's best scores in his later years, and another written by the composer for Dutch director Paul Verhoeven. On my blog, I wrote the review for this score after seeing the first *Fifty Shades of Grey* movie. For this book, I have deleted any comparison between these two erotic movies except for just one paragraph.

### The movie

*Basic Instinct* is a movie that would never be possible today. I am sure it would cause so much trouble that it would not have been released. When Paul Verhoeven was directing it, *Basic Instinct* caused a lot of trouble among gay and lesbian rights activists and demonstrators who found the movie offensive. They thought it was offending them, "thought" being the right word because there is not a single line in the script or the movie that could be considered as causing offence. The movie did offend a lot of people, but not gays and lesbians. The San Francisco police of were present every day of the shoot. I lived in San Francisco for two years and am familiar with the very hard-core liberal atmosphere there, but liberal also means accepting other opinions even when they do not match our own views.

Jerry Goldsmith commented the controversy: "This is one of the best pictures I've worked on in a long time, especially because Paul Verhoeven was so faithful to the script. It's very artistic and accessible, and all the surrounding debates are a bunch of cheap shots that have nothing to do with what the film is about. People are just trying to get a free ride off of it."[71]

Even before living in San Francisco I loved this movie, and for me *Basic Instinct* is still one of the best erotic thrillers ever made. If you compare it with recent erotic movies such as *Fifty Shades of Grey*, you can see how good Paul Verhoeven's movie is. I saw *Fifty Shades* with a female friend of mine, and other than being impressed by Dakota Johnson, did not very enjoy it. Back in my apartment, I grabbed the soundtrack of *Basic Instinct* and enjoyed listening to its dynamic music.

*Basic Instinct* was only Jerry Goldsmith and Paul Verhoeven's second collaboration, but because of their huge success with *Total Recall*, fans of the composer and the director were looking forward to it. The script was written by Joe Eszterhas, a terrific writer. If you ever have time to read his autobiography *Hollywood Animal*, do. It is a fabulous book about day-to-day business in Hollywood. I suppose the book gave away too much inside information because Eszterhas was not as active afterwards. What especially touched me was Eszterhas's honesty throughout the book and his fight cancer battle. The screenplay, written in the 1980s, was popular enough to prompt a bidding war; it was finally purchased by Carolco Pictures for a reported $3 million. Eszterhas wrote the film in 13 days.

A great many famous actors such as Al Pacino, Harrison Ford, Wesley Snipes, Robert De Niro, Mel Gibson, Bruce Willis and Sylvester Stallone were considered for the role of Nick Curran. I have read that in preparation for the car chase scene, Michael Douglas drove up the steps on Kearny Street in San Francisco for four nights by himself. I also heard that Douglas recommended Kim Basinger for the role of Catherine Tramell, but she declined it, as did Julia Roberts, Meg Ryan, Michelle Pfeiffer, Kathleen Turner and Ellen Barkin. Demi Moore was considered by Verhoeven before Sharon Stone was eventually selected for the role. She and Verhoeven had worked together on *Total Recall* so it made sense.

In *Hollywood Animal*, Eszterhas explained that he was willing to make changes to the script after the protests, but Verhoeven did not want that and explained in an interview that he was fighting for the authenticity of the script against the author, a crazy situation. In the liner notes to the complete soundtrack of the score, you can read more about what happened. When the director "tried to add an unnecessary lesbian sex scene [just for my understanding: what does unnecessary here mean?, SR] to the film and the writer, Joe Eszterhas, complained about it, Verhoeven told him that he was the director and Eszterhas the writer, so he was right and the writer was wrong, Eszterhas had to be physically restrained and vowed never to go near the director again. However, when Verhoeven eventually realised that the scene wouldn't work, he apologised to Eszterhas so humbly and unreservedly that the writer's view shifted from sheer hatred to complete admiration."
[72]

I am a big fan of Verhoeven, and after *Total Recall* this is the second review of a score for one of his movies in my book. It is sad that he is no longer working as a director on any big Hollywood movie right now. All his movies are crazy in a good way, and while watching *Showgirls* (1995) I can remember not being sure whether I should be shocked or more entertained by the totally serious approach to giving an inside view of showbiz in Las Vegas and in contrast the sometimes totally ridiculous scenes.

The pool sex scene ranks quite high as one of the most ridiculous sex scenes ever seen on screen. *Starship Troopers* (1997) was a very violent movie. It was so raw and brutal that people did not understand its satirical element. *Hollow Man* (2000), again with a score by Jerry Goldsmith, was mainstream entertainment but in a really good way, and you will have to examine Verhoeven's later non-Hollywood movies *Black Book* (2006) and *Elle* (2016) for yourself. I wish Verhoeven would come back to Hollywood and offer us another entertaining movie like *RoboCop* or *Basic Instinct*.

## The music

For Jerry Goldsmith, *Basic Instinct* was the first erotic thriller for which he would compose the music. There is a complete soundtrack edition of the music with 26 tracks, and I will discuss a few tracks here. Before I bought this edition, I had the original album, and even on this the score made a great impression on me with its seducing main theme and the haunting atmosphere Goldsmith created.

The composer described the musical direction: "Though it has graphic scenes, I'd describe BASIC INSTINCT as a sensuous thriller. This isn't about ordinary sex, so the music had to be erotic and evil at the same lime. I ended up writing three different themes, before I settled on one."[73]

So, I will start with the *Main Title,* which introduces the haunting main theme. It was funny to watch the audience reaction during this scene when I saw the movie in the cinema. I knew what was happening, but most of the audience did not, so people were shocked. The music reflects this shocking scene brilliantly. The percussion transforms the violence of the stabbing into music.

In my opinion, this kind of music works much better than Jerry Goldsmith's murder music in the sequel to *Psycho* from 1983.

Even though *Basic Instinct* is an erotic thriller, the sex which is shown is not shown in a pleasant way. Therefore, the music is not composed in the typical sex scene music style from the 1980s with strings and sax. For Verhoeven, sex is a battle between genders, it is a fight and it is aggressive, and so is Goldsmith's music.

*Pillow Talk* is the music for the first sex scene between Douglas and Stone. The music underscores the scene perfectly. Goldsmith builds up the tension first, the kind of music not expected for a sex scene, more for a suspense or murder mystery. The strings do not give you the pleasant feeling you expect from music for a scene like that. Goldsmith then transforms the sex rhythm into forwarding-thrusting music until you hear the release of ... all the tension.

If you are ever looking for a Jerry Goldsmith *Psycho* score in terms of a score creating an ice-cold and neurotic atmosphere other than the original by Bernard Herrmann, then it is not Goldsmith's score for the *Psycho* sequel you are looking for, but *Basic Instinct.* Like Herrmann, Goldsmith used the strings as the main instruments, but also woodwind and piano to create the haunting film noir feeling.

*Night Life* is played when Douglas is following Stone through the city. I am curious about what it was like for Michael Douglas to return to San Francisco in another policeman role after becoming famous for his cop role in the famous TV series *The Streets of San Francisco*.

This chase scene in *Basic Instinct* is a game of cat and mouse, and the music reflects this by balancing the quieter parts with the suddenly erupting action music. Listen in particular to how Goldsmith uses the percussion while the strings push the music forwards. The scene is beautifully shot, showing significant parts of San Francisco and the Bay Area.

The best action track is *Roxy Loses*. What a wonderful piece of music! Nearly four minutes long, this music is a perfect example of how to write an action piece and build suspense. Goldsmith uses the strings and the piano again to create a haunting atmosphere. The audience therefore knows that something is going to happen soon, and when Roxy suddenly attacks Douglas with her car, the music erupts.

Jerry Goldsmith composed a fabulous action piece, not as sophisticated as in his earlier scores from the 1970s, but *Basic Instinct* is not a movie for sophisticated underscoring. The movie is sometimes very rough, brutal and violent, and the music reflects all this. *She's Really Sick* is another example of excellent action scoring for a surprising and shocking scene.

The last track, *An Unending Story*, is also one of the best and nearly 10 minutes long. I love how Goldsmith uses the trumpets at the beginning to express Douglas's situation of solitude and emotional destruction. The piano is again used to build up a haunting atmosphere before Goldsmith underscores another passionate sex scene. This last track is a fabulous piece of music, with a dramaturgical structure you have to admire, and wonderfully orchestrated.

Jerry Goldsmith described it as one of his most challenging projects: *Basic Instinct* was "probably the most difficult I've ever done. It's a very convoluted story with very unorthodox characters. It's a murder mystery, but it isn't really a murder mystery. The director, Paul Verhoeven, had a very clear idea of how the woman should be, and I had a hard time getting it. Because of Paul pushing me, I think it's one of the best scores I've ever written. It was a true collaboration."[74]

If you compare this movie with *Fifty Shades of Grey*, you can see the difference. *Fifty Shades of Grey* is the sex movie for the present days, and Christian Grey is symptomatic of the male character in most of these movies. He has been emotionally hurt by a "Mrs Robinson" and is therefore not able to have a normal sexual relationship. Holy crap! So this guy is not even dominant or a sadist, he is acting like a hurt animal fighting for his life. Grey pretends to be a strong character but he is emotionally weak, and even though the woman is a virgin and shy, she is the strong one. *Fifty Shades* is a feminist movie and perhaps that kind of erotic film we need these days: a rich man, hurt in the past, looking for a woman who can heal him. That might be the dream of a lot of women these days.

In contrast *Basic Instinct* is a crazy weird movie with characters that immediately captivate you, a fabulous cast and Sharon Stone as a new sex symbol. The movie is wonderfully photographed by the German Jost Vacano (who also worked on Wolfgang Petersen's 1981 WWII classic *Das Boot*) and based on a script by one of the best thriller script authors. *Hollywood Animal* states that Eszterhas was not happy overall with the direction in which Paul Verhoeven pushed the story. Without doubt, Jerry Goldsmith's score is a masterpiece and sets the benchmark for music for erotic thrillers.

## III. Epilogue

*Basic Instinct* is the final review in this book. You may have reached the end of my book, but not the end of the amazing world of film music and soundtracks.

One day before finishing the re-writing of *Basic Instinct* for this publication, I watched *Murder on the Orient Express* (2017), Kenneth Branagh's adaptation of Agatha Christie's classic novel with a score by Patrick Doyle and an astonishing song sung by Michelle Pfeiffer. What a fantastic piece of music! I have not included this score in my book, but have talked about other Patrick Doyle scores which in my opinion are better.

This book has focused on Jerry Goldsmith's scores because he is my favourite film music composer. At film music concerts at the Barbican in London and talking to other film music enthusiasts, I have discovered that so many fans highly rate scores by Hans Zimmer, James Horner, John Williams and more recently Michael Giacchino. But Jerry Goldsmith? Often, I would be the first to mention his name.

Therefore, this book is also intended to promote his scores a little more and convince the conductors of film music concerts to include his music in their programmes more than they do. I am not getting any promotion fees for this! This is just a fan speaking.

If you agree or disagree with my collection in this book, have any comments to make or want to share your love of a particular soundtrack with me, I would be delighted to hear from you on my Facebook page (https://www.facebook.com/amazingmoviemusic/) or directly on my blog at www.amazingmoviemusic.com

When I first started collecting soundtracks, I never expected that I would start a blog of film music reviews, let alone publish a book about them. But by doing so, I have rediscovered the amazing world of soundtracks and film music and realised that if fans are still talking about composers, they will never be forgotten.

So, let's all go back to our CD players and listen to one of our much loved soundtracks again!

Guess which one I'm going to be listening to…

[1] Jerry Goldsmith in the liner notes to the soundtrack album.

[2] Jerry Goldsmith in the liner notes.

[3] Bill Conti in the liner notes to *North and South*. All following quotes from there.

[4] The composer in the lines notes.

[5] Again: the liner notes.

[6] Nick Redman in the liner notes to the Deluxe Edition of the score.

[7] Nick Redman in the liner notes.

[8] Patrick Doyle in the liner notes to the CD of the music.

[9] Patrick Doyle in the liner notes.

[10] https://www.nytimes.com/1994/11/04/movies/film-review-frankenstein-a-brain-on-ice-a-dead-toad-and-voila.html

[11] Christopher Husted in the liner notes to the CD release of *North by Northwest*, conducted by the composer. I highly recommend buying this full-length recording because with 50 tracks it offers the most complete CD of the music, and is conducted by the composer himself, which is very important especially in Herrmann's case for the tempi.

[12] Same liner notes.

[13] George Korngold in the liner notes to *The Adventures Of Robin Hood*.

[14] Lines Notes.

[15] Lines Notes.

[16] Lines Notes.

[17] Liner notes.

[18] Liner notes.

[19] Liner notes.

[20] http://www.filmtracks.com/titles/romancing_stone.html

[21] "Go ahead, pinko liberals, make my day. David D'Arcy meets John Milius, Hollywood's right-wing, cigar-chomping, gun-toting mover and shaker https://www.theguardian.com/film/2001/nov/08/artsfeatures

[22] Robert Townson in the liner notes to the Deluxe Edition of *The Omen*.

[23] But I found help on Wikipedia.

[24] Scott Timberg: "Bewitched again by John Updike", LA Times (September 20, 2009), http://articles.latimes.com/2009/sep/20/entertainment/ca-eastwick20

[25] Same article.

[26] Some fans may argue that this accolade should also go to Akiko Wakabayashi in *You Only Live Twice* (1967), Diana Rigg in *On Her Majesty's Secret Service* (1969) or Barbara Bach in *The Spy who Loved Me* (1977), but in my opinion only Lois Chiles's role is entirely convincing.

[27] More on Wikipedia.

[28] More on Wikipedia.

[29] More on Wikipedia.

[30] Quoted from Wikipedia. I could not find any internet link to this interview so I have to quote it from Wikipedia.

[31] Also found on Wikipedia.

[32] Patrick Doyle in the liner notes to the *Needful Things* CD.

[33] *Independence Day*. Filmtracks. 24 September 1996.

[34] A great resource for this work can be found at http://www.mfiles.co.uk/ composers/Elmer-Bernstein-an-overview-by-Jeffrey-Dane.htm

[35] Same website.

[36] Christopher Palmer in the liner notes to *Psycho* (the complete music for Alfred Hitchcock's classic suspense thriller).

[37] Same liner notes.

[38] Same liner notes.

[39] Same liner notes.

[40] Same liner notes.

[41] Here is an article about him:
https://www.express.co.uk/news/uk/386446/Trumpet-player-Watkins-dies-at-68

[42] Kirk Douglas mention some interesting facts about this movie in his autobiography *The Ragman's Son* (1988), a book I can highly recommend!

[43] http://www.filmtracks.com/titles/backdraft.html

[44] http://collider.com/michael-giacchino-on-jurassic-world-star-trek-3-and-more

[45] Quote from the Wikipedia article on *Total Recall*.

[46] http://www.runmovies.eu/jerry-goldsmith-on-scoring-basic-instinct/

[47] More can be learned about the production history and Williams's music on Wikipedia.

[48] Morrell wrote in 2000 an introduction to the novel (*Rambo and Me*) and gave an insight into the inspirations and development of the novel.

[49] Douglass Fake in the liner notes to the first complete original motion picture soundtrack of *First Blood*.

[50] https://www.thedailybeast.com/emma-stone-on-the-romantic-la-la-land-young-people-have-fallen-into-a-lot-of-cynicism

[51] Same interview.

[52] http://www.dailymail.co.uk/tvshowbiz/article-1104667/My-magnificent-seven-The-outrageous-memoirs-Hollywood-legend-Robert-Vaughn.html

[53] You can find more background information in John Cawley's *The Animated Films by Don Bluth*, http://www.cataroo.com/DBtail.html

[54] Jon Burlingame in the liner notes to the soundtrack CD of *Poltergeist* from 1982.

[55] Steven Spielberg in the liner notes.

[56] http://variety.com/2015/artisans/production/composer-patrick-doyle-creates-many-moods-for-cinderella-score-1201454740/ - also for the quotes that follow.

[57] John Williams in the liner notes to the extended CD of the soundtrack.

[58] Roger Spottiswoode in the liner notes to the Japan CD of *Under Fire*.

[59] Liner notes.

[60] Roberts, Jerry (8 September 1995). "Tapping a rich vein of gold; Jerry Goldsmith's music is as varied as the films he's scored". Daily Variety.

[61] Commentary to *Star Trek: The Motion Picture Directors Edition* [Disc 2].

[62] Christopher Nolan in the liner notes to *Interstellar*.

[63] Christopher Nolan in the liner notes.

[64] Christopher Nolan.

[65] Liner notes.

[66]http://www.hollywoodreporter.com/news/composer-hans-zimmer-talks-interstellar-745891

[67] Hans Zimmer in the liner notes.

[68] Liner notes.

[69] Liner notes.

[70]    https://www.polygon.com/2018/5/22/17380048/solo-star-wars-donald-glover-lando-calrissian-pansexual

[71] Jerry Goldsmith in an interview with Daniel Schweiger
(http://www.runmovies.eu/jerry-goldsmith-on-scoring-basic-instinct).

[72] Gary Kester in the liner notes. Please correct the name of the classical composer in the liner notes: it is Bruckner not Brueckner, and twice mocking a non-English speaker's way of speaking English is not very nice.

[73] Jerry Goldsmith with Daniel Schweiger.

[74] Velez, Andy. "Evening the Score" Jerry Goldsmith interview. Barnes & Noble. Retrieved 2011-06-06.

CPSIA information can be obtained
at www.ICGtesting.com
Printed in the USA
LVHW040907170422
716424LV00005B/863